THE
EQUIPPING
MINISTRY

by Paul Benjamin

Prevalent methods of one-minister churches will fail to evangelize the world. Here is a Bible-based plan by which this generation of Christians can reach this generation of the unsaved.

STANDARD PUBLISHING

Cincinnati, Ohio   4037

Library of Congress Catalog Card No. 76-53152

ISBN: 0-87239-164-7

**American Church Growth Study Series
National Church Growth Research Center
Box 3760 Washington, D. C. 20007**

To my mother,
Ada E. Benjamin

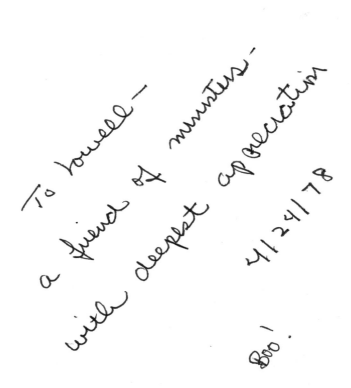

To Lowell —
a friend of ministers —
with deepest appreciation

4/24/78

Boo!

PREFACE

The church has always had many doctors for its ills. It is doubtful, however, if any single diagnosis and/or prescription is comprehensive enough to give a clean bill of health to the ailing bride of Christ.

We here passionately protest the way the American church uses and abuses its preaching ministry. While the kingdom languishes for want of dynamic leadership, a prophetic race has been reduced to "hewers of wood and drawers of water" for the congregation.

This malady will not find its cure in any denial of servanthood by church leaders. Better health will be restored, however, when church leadership functions scripturally—preparing and equipping others for the work of the ministry in the church.

This is the prescription indicated. The Biblical role of the preaching ministry must be restored. At the same time, the people in the pews must be freed to become the ministers of Jesus Christ which God has always intended.

The equipping ministry is not a miracle drug, some kind of a cure-all for problems in the church. But it is my studied conviction that the world will never hear the gospel preached without it.

Because the terminology in American churches is so varied, it is difficult to find terms which everyone uses and understands. The titles "pastor," "preacher," "minister," "parson," "elder," evangelist," and others, are all employed to designate the person who leads the congregation and usually delivers the sermons. Consequently I have used *preaching minister* throughout this study. It is the designation which I feel will be most fully understood by the greatest number of people. At times I have used the term "layman," while recognizing that the New Testament makes no "clergy-laity" distinction so familiar in the religious world today.

Some folk are uneasy with the word *equipping*, because they feel it has a kind of metallic or materialistic ring to it. One can talk about "equipping an army," or "equipping a ball team." According to Webster's Unabridged Dictionary, the word *equipping* carries the idea of "making ready or competent for service or action." I have used the word, of course, in this latter sense. This concept, I believe, is true to the meaning of the apostle Paul when he speaks in Ephesians of "the equipment of the saints for the work of the ministry."

This study suggests a bold approach to the equipping ministry. It asks the preaching minister and the congregation to work through the whole concept together. Changes from the traditional kind of one-person ministry, prevalent in the average congregation, can then be gradually initiated. Even one or two people, working quietly in the background, could start to make necessary changes. Any action which helps unlock the tremendous unused resources in a congregation will be a positive move in the right direction. I believe in the reasonableness of Christian people and I trust their basic instincts to want to do right. I therefore feel that a study of this nature will prompt changes in attitudes and behavior which could revolutionize the Christian ministry.

Time is of the essence for such change. I believe the church needs to act decisively today. God-given opportunities must be seized now. He has promised the victory.

This book is a part of the American Church Growth Study Series, which now includes *The Growing Congregation* and *How in the World?* Study guides for group discussion are also available.

CONTENTS

INTRODUCTION

For over two years, I have read and reread what the Scriptures say about the equipping ministry. It has been a rewarding experience.

I am indebted to other writers who have also explored the concept of the ministry of all believers. Some are voices from the pew. They are often frustrated with the "clergy" and the church. Others, from the pulpit, decry the lack of spiritual concern which they feel characterizes the average American Christian.

I have tried to present a balanced view, hoping that honesty and fairness will open the way for the Holy Spirit to deal afresh with all of us. My own experience in both the pulpit and the pew of American churches has, I trust, afforded me an objective viewpoint.

Some of my friends have been among my most helpful critics. Much of their input may be found in the Appendix, in the section titled "References and Comments." They have read the manuscript and have given me their suggestions. Several gave me four or five pages of single-spaced comments. Sometimes the response was a paragraph or two about a particular point.

Others responded by long-distance telephone call at their own expense. Without their contributions, this whole study would be greatly impoverished. Below is a list of those who have responded at the time of this writing:

Paul W. Anderson	Wilbur R. Aten
William Anderson	James O. Baird
Ben Armstrong	Harold Bales
Win Arn	Dale Baldwin
J. Spencer Arnold	Charles W. Barner

M. Wendell Belew
Lois Benjamin
Kenneth E. Bennett
✓ Lowell W. Berry
George W. BonDurant
Vonette Bright
Frederick T. Burkey
John D. Castelein
Ernest H. Chamberlain
Bob Chitwood
Robert E. Coleman
Ronald W. Collins
Clyde Cook
Donald S. Cox
James M. Cunningham
Richard R. DeRidder
Julia Doyle
Joe S. Ellis
David L. Eubanks
Roy J. Fish
Leighton Ford
James W. Greenwood
Tillman Habegger
Joe Hale
Earl C. Hargrove
Olin W. Hay
James P. Henry
C. Curtis Hess
Richard D. Hogan
C. B. Hogue
Glenn E. Hull
Dale D. Jacobs

Gordon G. Johnson
Medford E. Jones
Erwin J. Kolb
Charles W. Koller
Nate Krupp
Nathaniel Linsey
W. F. Lown
Donald A. McGavran
Ford Madison
Kenneth A. Meade
Matthew M. Meyer
Carl W. Moorhous
George Morris
Larry O. Osborne
Woodrow Phillips
Henry B. Pratt
Walter Puckett
T. A. Raedeke
Robert Shell
Frank S. Smith
Rondal B. Smith
Tom A. Smith
Carl William Somers
G. H. J. Thibodeaux
Lamar Tillman
James C. Vaughn
Ronald L. Walters
Timothy M. Warner
John Wesley White
Earl A. Wood
Ruth Wood
Robert F. Yawberg

To all these, and to many others, I am extremely grateful.

UNDERSTANDING
THE EQUIPPING MINISTRY

the basic idea

What is the equipping ministry? How does it differ from more traditional concepts of ministry? How does a preaching minister change his style of leadership? What may be learned from New Testament models of ministry? Why is the equipping ministry so important?

The purpose of this study is to answer these and other significant questions related to the ministry of Christ's church. Actions are directly motivated by our concepts. If our understanding is accurate, then our behavior can be altered to reflect our comprehension.

Many congregations have never examined their thinking regarding the role of a preaching minister in light of New Testament teaching. Through tradition and practice, they have formed a general idea about the way a "good" minister functions. If the present preaching minister conforms to their ideas about the ministry, then he is welcome to remain with the congregation. On the other hand, if his style of ministry is not acceptable, he must change his ways or move to a new field of service.

Such practice never deals with the root of the problem. Suppose both the preaching minister and the congregation have a faulty attitude about the way he should function. Then what? Who is to blame? If alterations are needed, who will initiate them? Furthermore, how can they decide whose views are correct?

Our basic concept of leadership in the church must come from the Scripture. *Most congregations today employ a paid leader to minister for them, whereas in the New Testament, the primary purpose of a leadership ministry is to equip the congregation to minister* (Ephesians 4:11).

This book calls for a very important turnaround in the thinking of the average church. Some in the congregation will respond with a "ho hum" or "so what." On the other hand, those who really care about the mission of Christ through the church will see this fundamental shift in thinking as extremely vital. It is one of the basic keys to church growth and world evangelization. It is also a critical step toward congregational harmony and outreach.

the equipping ministry of Jesus

The essential concept of ministry in the church stems from the life and work of Jesus himself. " 'The Son of man,' " He said, " 'came not to be served but to serve' " (Mark 10:45). This summary statement is very important in any study of the equipping ministry.

Although the accounts in the four Gospels are tantalizingly brief, we know that Jesus practiced an equipping kind of leadership on earth. How did He go about it? First of all, He found others to minister. "He found Philip," John records, "and said to him, 'Follow me' " (1:43). Jesus continued to discover others who could minister. Some turned away because they would not meet the stringent demands of work in the kingdom (Luke 9:57-62).

Jesus equipped others to minister by loving them (John 13:1), by teaching them (Matthew 5:2), by praying for them (Luke 22:39-41), and by training them on the job (Matthew 10:5ff, Luke 10:1ff).

The preparation of ministers was a major concern of Jesus. Why? Could He not be satisfied with the spectacular results of His own work? Thousands followed Him from place to place. He could scarcely find time to sleep or eat. Sometimes it was necessary for Him to flee from the multitudes. His name became a household word. Why then did He call others to service?

Consider the purpose of the relationship of Jesus with His disciples. Of course, they enjoyed His masterful teaching. Of course, there were lazy days on the Sea of Galilee with great fellowship and laughter. Of course, He loved them and they loved Him. They were His friends (John 15:15). But the purpose of it all—what was the purpose of it all?

The mission of the twelve and of the seventy gives us a clue. Matthew says, "These twelve Jesus sent out" (10:5). Luke writes, "After this the Lord appointed seventy others, and sent them on ahead of him" (10:1). They were called to be sent. Here we have a significant key to the ministry of Jesus. He equipped others to perform a ministry of their own.

the equipping ministry of Paul

The apostle Paul also practiced an equipping ministry. Some are prone to think of the great missionary to the Gentiles as a "lone eagle," traveling in solitude throughout the Mediterranean basin with his message of salvation. What are the facts?

Actually, Paul carried on a kind of "walking seminary" throughout his missionary journeys. He surrounded himself with those who could later go out on their own. At Lystra, he found Timothy to accompany him (Acts 16:3). Later, Luke recorded that others had been enlisted in the Pauline band: "Sopater of Beroea, the son of Phyrrhus, accompanied him; and of the Thessalonians, Aristarchus and Secundus; and Gaius of Derbe, and Timothy; and the Asians, Tychicus and Trophimus" (Acts 20:4).

Here was a small congregation Paul took with him as he traveled. Later Crescens and Demas joined the group, along with others. Mark, who started with him on the first journey and went home, later returned to the work. After mentioning Demas who deserted the cause, Paul wrote, "Crescens has gone to Galatia, Titus to Dalmatia. Luke alone is with me. Get Mark and bring him with you; for he is very useful in serving me. Tychicus I have sent to Ephesus" (2 Timothy 4:10-12).

These Scriptures indicate the kind of equipping ministry which Paul practiced. He found potential leaders as he traveled from city to city. In many cases, they were invited to accompany him, and they learned as they traveled. Later on, they were directed to their own place of ministry. Paul was true to the "equipping concept" which he sets forth in Ephesians 4:11.

In his writing, Paul kept in mind those whom he was equipping for ministry. He insisted that Timothy pay strict attention to "scripture" since it is "profitable for teaching, for reproof, for correction, and for training in righteousness, that the man of God may be complete, *equipped* for every good work" (2 Timothy 3:16).

The church will always be in debt to Barnabas who helped sponsor Paul in his early ministry. Shunned by the disciples because they knew his reputation for persecuting Christians, Paul found in Barnabas the mentor he needed in his rise to leadership. This incident points up a real test of the equipping ministry. What happens when we recruit those whose abilities eclipse our own? Do we encourage them, or seek to thwart them in their mission?

adjusting to the concept

In order for a congregation to begin operating on the principles of the equipping ministry, some adjustments will be necessary.

A historian remarked about Woodrow Wilson that he "made no fetish of the god of things-as-they-are." Those who are satisfied with the concept of ministry now held by the majority of American congregations will not be interested in changing. On the other hand, Christians who are feeling frustrated and defeated by our present system of ministry will welcome a more Scriptural approach.

Every preaching minister needs to know where he stands in his own thinking regarding the equipping concept. He must realize the different nature of this procedure. He cannot lead the congregation on a pilgrimage when he is unsure of his own direction. Hazy thinking on his part is certain to be sensed and reflected throughout the church.

Sometimes a preaching minister feels a non-equipping ministry will work in the congregation if he tries harder and puts in more hours. When the basic concept itself is faulty, however, then change must be made on a deeper level.

Fundamental to our thinking must be the New Testament precept and precedent—*every Christian is a minister of Jesus Christ*. Peter refers to his readers as a "royal priesthood" and calls them to the responsibility of declaring "the wonderful deeds of him who called you out of the darkness into his marvelous light" (1 Peter 2:9). In the book of Revelation, John spoke about the ascended Christ who has "made us a kingdom, priests to his God and Father" (1:6). The idea of every Christian being a minister for Christ is finally dawning upon the American church. During a long night, growth has been thwarted by the "one minister-one congregation" concept of ministry.

Faced with the advent of an equipping ministry, some preaching ministers experience an identity crisis. "If everyone is a minister," they reason, "then what is important for me to do?" They ask, "What distinctive role do I have with a congregation?"

Such questions are understandable. The work of the preaching minister takes on new lustre, however, when he is fulfilling his rightful vocation. He is the one who has usually received special training for his work. He is a "professional" in the best sense of the word. There will always be the need for a paid career ministry in the church.

His work is to set about helping others in the congregation to minister. He must know something about the spiritual qualifications and the capabilities of each person he "equips." When he knows the people, and loves them for their own worth, he can begin preparing them for their ministry.

The equipping ministry, properly conducted, will incorporate both Biblical and sociological principles of leadership. It is not a leadership-leveling process. Every person has a different degree of leadership. A shared leadership within the church is certainly a Biblical concept, but the idea of "equal influence" is not. Some have more influence than others. Paul had more influence than Barnabas. Peter, James, and John evidently had the most leadership ability among the twelve. The writer of Hebrews is not contradicting the concept of the equipping ministry when he admonishes his readers to "remember your leaders, those who spoke to you the word of God" (13:7).

It is taken for granted that a preaching minister (or preaching ministers) will have a marked influence on the life of a church. The important thing is how he uses such influence. Some ministers walk softly at first, then later carry a "big stick." Once they have control, woe to the person who opposes them on any detail! Their will reigns supreme.

In a time of war, Congress grants the President of the United States almost dictatorial powers. When the crisis is over, however, the same Congress redistributes these powers. The nation's founding fathers saw the dangers of a government without checks and balances.

This principle is applicable to the church. Paul evidently entrusted Titus with some very strong powers in Crete (Titus 1:5). It is foolish to assume, though, that Paul is here repealing the New Testament procedure of selecting church leadership with the aid of the congregation (Acts 6:3).

The preaching minister who is accustomed to making all decisions must gradually begin to relinquish some authority to others. A "ruling elder" may need to do the same. Members of the congregation who have been mere passive sheep must become active with the shepherds in "building up the body of Christ" (Ephesians 4:12).

Early attempts to perform an equipping ministry for a congregation may be checked by "starts" and "stops." Such dramatic change will not happen overnight. Churches must have time to adjust to the new style of leadership. The equipping ministry, however, when accepted and implemented by the church, will unleash new impetus for the gospel which most of us have only dreamed about. It can change the world.

REASONS FOR REFOCUS

the impossible burden

Dozens of young ministers become disillusioned and disenchanted with the ministry in their first few years of service. Their idealism is shattered. What happens to them? What is happening in the congregations they served?

Some would answer, "If the average minister gave more attention to organization, worked more diligently, and if he dedicated himself more completely to God, then he could emerge triumphant in the local church situation." An objective study of the New Testament, however, reveals that our basic system of ministry has been largely at fault.

Look for a moment at the current situation. The young minister leaves the college or seminary with the idea of accomplishing great things for God. He tries to adjust to the expectations which the congregation has for him. They want him to preach inspiring messages at every service. They expect him to visit the sick without fail. They rely upon him to lead out in raising finances. They expect him to keep up the attendance. They intend for him to be present for the social functions of the congregation. Also, they usually expect him to take an active part in community affairs.

What is the origin of all these ministerial expectations? For the most part, the job description of the preaching minister in America "just grew"! The first American ministers were largely of the circuit type. Many of them engaged in other occupations such as farming or trading.

They preached from place to place as they were invited. Later on, congregations began to form where the gospel was being preached. These congregations built meeting houses. Soon they were looking for a leader to serve as "their" minister. His role developed in response to the felt needs of the congregation. The worship service, the Sunday school, the funeral, the wedding, the sick bed, the family, the committee meeting—these all became areas for the minister's labors. Very few stopped long enough to ask for a Biblical definition of his role. Consequently, his performance was rated more on the basis of cultural expectations or church tradition than upon New Testament teaching.

The sum of extra-Scriptural expectations often places an unbearable burden on a minister. Some leaders, of course, are exceptional. They have physical and mental endowments which surpass the average. Some ministers are able to work sixteen hours a day, seven days a week. They seldom take a vacation. They are never sick. By extraordinary labors, they are able to thrive upon the one-man ministry concept. They seem to enjoy it. Their example, however, often places a heavier burden on others, less gifted, who cannot keep up their pace. Conscientious ministers who attempt to measure their own success by such extraordinary standards will forever feel like failures.

Most preaching ministers are sensitive human beings who want everyone's approval. Consequently, it becomes a shattering experience when they discover people in the congregation who dislike them. If they are married, their families suffer with them. Often, this dislike is related to their failure to live up to some misguided congregational expectation. Such hurts can develop into anger or despair. In many instances, they look for another vocation. The move from the parsonage then comes as a welcome relief to the entire family.

a frustrated congregation

While the preaching minister is feeling the burden of leadership for the congregation, members in the pews are frustrated in another way. They faithfully attend worship services Sunday after Sunday. Here they are exhorted, while seated row on row, to live better Christian lives, give more liberally to Christian causes, and be more faithful about attending church meetings.

It often seems that the purpose of attending church and Sunday school is to receive the weekly admonition to "attend church and Sunday school." Or, in a circular way, the morning service is the time to be exhorted to attend evening service; the evening service is the time to be exhorted to attend Wednesday night service; and the Wednesday night service is the time to be exhorted to attend Sunday morning service.

The patient people who sit through church services Sunday after Sunday have been referred to as "God's Frozen People." As Kraemer reminds us, "They exist as frozen assets and dead capital," seldom carrying out the work of the kingdom. Sometimes these people are spiritually downgraded by a preaching minister. He feels the members of the congregation should be more actively involved in Christian service. Here is the truth of the matter: the frightful unemployment rate in the church is often the fault of the minister himself. When people in the pews fail to participate more fully in congregational life, it is not always because they are uncommitted—it may be because they are uncalled and untrained.

The anesthetizing effects of repeated worship services Sunday after Sunday is well known. A congregation begins to operate under an illusion. Having been reminded so many times of their duty as Christians, the hearing itself is equated with the performance. Listening to a good sermon on evangelism becomes a substitute for evangelism. This attitude is described by the following clever lines:

They're praising God on Sunday.

They'll be all right on Monday.

It's just a little habit they've acquired.

Some congregations are frustrated because the preaching minister is constantly involving people in "busy work." Without consulting anyone, he keeps dreaming up ideas for everyone else to follow. Then, when people do not give him an enthusiastic response, he sometimes thunders at them from the pulpit or finds some more subtle way of expressing his disapproval.

To solve the problem of the overloaded minister, some congregations move into a multiple-staff situation. Yet, this solution too is inadequate outside the equipping-ministry context. In fact, adding more staff only makes it easier for a congregation to sit back while they pay others to minister for them. It often perpetuates the whole non-equipping system.

A growing congregation demands a growing number of professional leaders. Each staff member, however, should be involved in the equipping ministry. Whether a person serves in education, in music, in clerical work, in counseling, or in evangelism, one of the primary responsibilities of that area of service is to equip others.

At the same time, the potential task force of dedicated volunteers must not be overlooked. Some folks of retirement age in the congregation welcome a greater responsibility in the church. Many times they simply need a little instruction and some on-the-field training. Younger members are willing to become more deeply involved too if they are provided with a genuine opportunity to minister, and with adequate training.

the unfinished work

Jesus Christ is the "King of Concern" and His body, the church, should be a caring fellowship. Adolph Harnack, the German historian and theologian, cites the loving consideration of the early Christians for one another as most significant. He sees their deep affection and their willingness to help others in a time of crisis as a primary factor in impressing the pagans with the authenticity of their message.

Every phase of human life produces its own particular set of needs. The young marrieds need strong and stable homes. Singles, who are often lonely and vulnerable to temptation, need the sense of a corporate family through the church. Because old age often creates a sense of uselessness and despair, retirees need the feeling of being wanted and useful.

Essential to the body upbuilding itself (Ephesians 4:11) is the idea of a mutual ministry within the body. One part of the body provides help for the other parts. For example, young people need wisdom for living. Older members, through their successes and failures, have a fund of wisdom to help them. Couples with troubled marriages can sometimes be helped by another couple who are succeeding in marriage.

As a Spanish proverb has it, "sooner or later, the *hush* comes to every home." Life is pocked by disease, invalidism, and finally death. When the *hush* comes, burden-bearing comes sharply into focus (Galatians 6:2).

So the work of a congregation ministering to itself is a gigantic task. The needs within a congregation are varied and constant. Every day brings with it new matters of concern. The preaching minister who attempts to serve all these needs alone can write above his office door: "The Work Here Is Never Done!"

Picture the typical congregation in America where two hundred people meet on Sunday morning for worship. Another two hundred members of this average church seldom attend worship or contribute financially. Some preaching ministers feel they have little responsibility for what they call the "inactives." A probable majority, however, feel that the non-attending two hundred also have a claim upon their ministry and upon the resources of the congregation.

Here is a group of four hundred people, equal to the population of a small village in the United States. Every boy and girl in the congregation has a special set of needs. Every family requires spiritual and/or other kinds of help at one time or another. In the one-minister church, how is it possible for all these areas of concern to be met adequately?

The tragedy, of course, is that the personal needs of individuals in the congregation are simply not being met. The high drop-out rate in American churches is well known. Most of these people are not angry with God. They still reverence the name of Jesus Christ. They have often left the institutional church due to apathy, boredom, or neglect.

Perhaps they suffered in the hospital for several weeks and no one from the congregation showed any concern.

They may have faced a marital crisis which provoked gossip rather than help.

Why is it that so many members of American congregations feel neglected? Some, of course, are merely seeking excuses to pursue their own worldly choices. Others are genuinely saddened because their church is so insensitive to their hurts. Sometimes the other members are cold and unfriendly.

The irony of the situation causes the thoughtful observer to weep. Thousands of maturing Christians in American congregations are seeking to become more useful in helping those who hurt. Thousands of others are desperately in need. Yet, such ministries of one-to-one benevolence are not happening.

Many preaching ministers openly confess their feelings of inadequacy. They see themselves as only skimming the tops of the waves. They want to give more time to sermon preparation, to their devotional life, to counseling, and to evangelistic calling. They often feel that they are neglecting their own families.

The solution to these dilemmas can come through the equipping ministry. The root of the problem lies in the fact that we are working the wrong way. Following the same practices with more fervor only compounds the problem. A basic reorientation for both the congregation and the preaching minister is desperately needed. Otherwise, the body will continue to suffer and the lost will not be found.

the community unevangelized

If the needs within the Christian community are immense, those outside are even greater. Millions of American young people are growing up without any kind of Christian teaching. The public schools, because of their religious-neutrality stance, usually provide little spiritual help for students. In fact, the influence often flows in the other direction. Meanwhile, American young people are taking their value systems from the current culture with its heavy overload of humanism, eroticism, and violence.

What should be our attitude toward these neglected millions? Who has time to minister to them? Conscientious leaders indict themselves over their failure to evangelize. Seeking and finding the lost for Christ is a time-consuming ministry. It often demands additional energy from the preaching minister which is simply not there. Yet, Augustine reminds us, "none is beloved unless known." How can we love a community whose people remain largely unknown to us?

Here again we see the absolute imperative for the total ministry of all believers. The equipping ministry requires preparation of others to evangelize. The work of evangelization can be accomplished only when the congregation of two hundred members has two hundred ministers for Christ!

Some in the congregation may be reluctant to evangelize because they feel their "gift" is lacking. It is very possible, of course, that they may lack the spiritual endowment to become a full-time evangelist. The Bible does say *"some evangelists"* (Ephesians 4:11). This verse, however, does not exclude the majority of Christians from being witnesses to their faith.

Many Christians know so little about their "gifts" because they are never given a chance to exercise them. On the other hand, hundreds of Christians have become effective witnesses for Christ who did not believe they had that ability. Some religious groups in this country are making converts by the tens of thousands, simply because they constantly stress the every-member-a-witness concept.

The evangelization of communities, let alone the world, is impossible within a clergy-laity system. There are simply not enough workers nor enough hours in the day. With an equipping ministry, however, millions of the unchurched can be reached for Christ.

MOVING TOWARD CHANGE

overcoming tradition

How do congregations, some of them with more than a century of tradition behind them, change their ways? We can all be understanding with those who have been reared with a particular point of view over the years. Change does not come easily.

When a young minister in one church tried to introduce the Biblical concept of the equipping ministry, he was criticized by a lady who had grown up in the parsonage. She became defensive in the situation, feeling that her father's style of leadership in the ministry was being put to trial.

Once the wheels of tradition are in motion for the average congregation, scarcely anyone asks who started them rolling. One congregation held an annual "homecoming" service. The purpose of this gathering was to welcome back those who had formerly been members. Even though in later years no one came who was not already an active, resident member, the church continued to have the service anyway. They had just forgotten what its purpose was.

One minister decided to continue seeking a pulpit until he found a church willing to adopt the equipping-ministry principle. After several months of looking, he met with a congregation whose leaders were enthusiastic about the idea. After he moved, however, and tried to implement the concept, the project failed. The change in practice was simply too radical. Even several long discussions with the church board were not sufficient to overcome the one-minister-one-church tradition.

Every congregation operates by certain internal principles, some of which are unconscious and unexamined. People may even have difficulty putting these ideas into words, despite the fact that such unwritten laws may form the underlying policies for the entire program of the church. Unless the leadership is able to look at these views objectively, some false concepts may continue to govern the life of the congregation.

In order to adopt an equipping ministry, every congregation needs some kind of model to follow. It has been suggested that the seminary itself furnishes the congregation with an example. The professors in seminary are there for one primary purpose—equipping others to minister. The courses in Bible, theology, history, and the practical field, are all designed to prepare the students to minister. Chapel attendance and service projects are also part of the equipping process.

Can the model of the seminary be reproduced by the average congregation? Yes! The first step for a preaching minister is to prepare his own faculty of "equippers." Because of their longtime residence in the area, the members should be able to guide him with reference to the church and the community. Then, working together in a spirit of harmony and love, they can prepare the whole congregation to minister. The ministry of the Apostle Paul in Ephesus, and his subsequent address to the elders (Acts 20:17-38), is a case in point.

the gain in position

Some pulpit ministers strongly oppose the equipping ministry. Many of them fear it will curtail their influence and lower their position. Furthermore, the apparent success of some dictatorial ministers makes them question the validity of the whole concept. They have observed friends in the ministry being "unhorsed" in a congregational leadership struggle. Consequently, they have quietly vowed to remain always in the saddle and keep the reins in their own hands.

The preaching minister who opposes the equipping concept, however, is often unaware of its benefits. Most leaders want to be loved. Who has a firmer hold on the affections of people than the godly professor who is esteemed by his students? People will always have a warm and tender place in their heartrs for the one who helped them most.

The equipping minister is constantly gaining in influence as he leads individuals in the congregation toward their own meaningful ministry. He is not a "rule or ruin" type. Instead, he envisions how every member of the body can become more effective in the service of Jesus Christ. The church is more like a filling station than a reform school. It was Jeremiah whom the Lord reminded, "But seek the welfare of the city where I have sent you into exile, and pray to the Lord on its behalf, for in its welfare you will find your welfare" (Jeremiah 29:7).

From the standpoint of human nature, one of the basic needs of human beings is a feeling of self-worth. Parents who over-discipline their children may find out later, to their sorrow, that they have robbed their child of self-esteem. Nothing is more deadly to human happiness than a poor self-image. The equipping minister sees possibilities in others they never even visualize for themselves. By helping them find a meaningful ministry for

Christ instead of always contributing to his own ministerial success, the church acquires another worker who finds a higher self-esteem. At the same time, the preaching minister personally gains a lifelong friend.

The pulpit minister's influence begins to wane the day the congregation discovers he is a power-hungry manipulator. It is terribly distressing when a sincere young minister is bitten by the "power bug." His desire for more authority can never be satisfied. He often continues to do the right things and say the right words, but from the wrong motives. He may become too aware of his talents in the pulpit or of his bewitching way with people. Soon his remarkable talents turn inward for his own purposes and he becomes a thwarter rather than a servant in the kingdom.

Jesus repeatedly cautioned against the love of power among the twelve. When He washed the feet of the disciples, it was primarily a lesson for their humility (John 13:15). "Whoever would be great among you must be your servant" He reminded His disciples on the night of His betrayal (Mark 10:43). When Salome approached him about a position of prominence for her sons, He reminded her that wearing the crown requires bearing the cross (Matthew 20:20-28).

Jesus is not the kind of leader who demands the wills of others simply for the sake of dominating them. He did not freeze out those who thought and felt differently. But He did require His followers to give up lesser concerns for the sake of the kingdom of God (Luke 18:18-30).

expectations of the congregation

Congregations usually hold certain traditional expectations about the vocational activity of their preaching

minister. Even though such views may be more traditional than Biblical, they still have a tremendously bind-
ing force.

Many of these expectations are generated by the wish
for a "private chaplain." The preaching minister "be-
longs" to a particular congregation. They pay his salary
and furnish him a parsonage. His success or failure is
often measured by the degree to which he lives up to
unwritten assumptions which exist when he comes. His
family must fulfill preconceived images as well.

If, for example, a preaching minister accepts "too
many" speaking engagements out of town, he may be
questioned by the board. They may even resent the
number of invitations he receives. They fail to realize
their advantage in having a talented public speaker Sunday after Sunday. Only after he moves do they under-
stand their loss.

With the advent of the hospital in American society,
traditions have developed concerning the minister and
his hospital visits. Even though a large congregation may
have a staff of preaching ministers, people still want the
"senior" minister to call. A visit by the associate, or by
an elder, often will not suffice.

No minister with a compassionate heart wants to neglect people in the hospital. Yet this phase of his ministry
in many large congregations has come to have tremendous proportions. With several hundred members, he
may have patients in half a dozen hospitals, located as
much as a hundred miles apart. Energy and time are
lacking. What is the conscientious minister to do?

If the congregation has a multiple staff, the senior
minister can arrange for certain staff members to visit the
hospitals on particular days of the week. One preaching

minister says facetiously, "If you want me to call on you in the hospital, you'll have to get sick on Tuesday." Another way is to share this ministry with others in the congregation.

Some preaching ministers take apprentices from the congregation with them when they visit the sick. Often they encourage their helper to participate by reading the Scripture or praying. Later, they may ask this "new minister" to visit the sick and take a helper with him.

The equipping ministry is not a device whereby pulpit ministers escape their God-given responsibilities. Rather, it is a means by which they fulfill their Scriptural role. As it is, the fallacy of the one-man-minister concept becomes more apparent as congregational life becomes more complex. The situation can change only as congregations revise their ministerial expectations.

In addition to other values already emphasized, the equipping ministry guarantees the ongoing ministry of the congregation if the preaching minister is disabled or moves. Once he has trained others, their ministry will continue. The congregation will be strong and healthy in spite of such contingencies.

Neither congregation nor preaching minister lose by practicing equipping-ministry principles. Yet, human nature being what it is, some are bound to complain. What happens then? A preaching minister may be reluctant to cut against the grain of tradition, especially if his emotional security rests on receiving the affirmation of others. He may feel the pressure of a neighboring minister who is having great "success" in more traditional ways. At times, he may feel very lonely in his pursuit. He will need the courage of his convictions and, if he is married, an understanding family.

One cannot always predict the way people will respond. The man who is the stingiest during a financial campaign for current expenses, may later leave his entire estate to the church. Otherwise disinterested youth may become excited over an in-depth Bible study or a prayer breakfast. Human nature cannot be second-guessed.

some who will not change

Even allowing for surprises, however, some people simply will not change, at least not without resistance. Storms may lie ahead for the congregation which chooses to adopt an equipping ministry. Many Americans are still comfortable with the idea that following Christ requires one hour in weekly worship and a small donation. They are not interested in additional opportunities for investing their time and energies in eternal values. Consequently, to speak of the "ministry of all believers" elicits a negative or half-hearted response.

A minister persuaded the members of one congregation to conduct a witness-survey of a new community. During the survey one lady remarked to several others, "Why are we out here doing the preacher's work?" Obviously she missed the whole point of all the teaching she was receiving.

We are usually influenced far more by what we feel than by what we think. Some church members have an emotional block about the whole equipping idea. An appeal to reason does not reach their will since the decision is being made in another area of their psyche.

It is probably better to follow a more traditional pattern of ministry for a while, if bitterness and strife break out in the congregation. Most people need time to adjust. A pulpit minister may lose his influence with a church because he has moved too far too fast. People need time to work a new idea through their own mental processes.

If insurmountable tensions arise, perhaps the preaching minister should move elsewhere. It is better to remove himself from the scene than to stay with a congregation of unhappy and resentful people. It is also possible that a new personality in the pulpit will encounter less resistance to a new program.

LIBERATION FOR ALL

new opportunities for ministry

The equipping ministry relieves the preaching minister of a tremendous psychological burden. One of the greatest anxieties among ministers today is the fear of failure. The finger of responsibility is often pointed toward the pulpit when the congregational shortcomings occur. If the attendance lags, if the budget is short, if someone in the hospital is overlooked, if the church bulletin has an error, usually the preaching minister takes the blame.

It does not take very many of these criticisms from the congregation for a preaching minister to feel he may have missed his calling. A lack of congregational approval often leaves him with a sense of loneliness. If he is married, his family shares the pain. Soon discouragement takes its toll and another effective Christian leader finds a place in business.

In the equipping ministry, however, responsibility is mutually shared. The lack of numerical growth, unmet budgets, or inaccurate announcements become corporate problems, not just individual ones. The congregation asks the question, "What are *we* going to do about these problems?"

The key to survival for the preaching minister is his selectivity regarding his responsibilities. Paul's instructions to Timothy and Titus carried a reminder for them to emphasize their preaching and teaching ministry. He wrote Timothy, "Attend to the public reading of scripture, to preaching, to teaching" (1 Timothy 4:13). He told Titus, "Teach what befits sound doctrine" (Titus 2:1).

Most congregations today place a premium on their preaching minister's work in the pulpit. Yet, good sermonizing and constant running from place to place are generally incompatible. One preaching minister told a new congregation they could have either his head or his feet, but they could not have both.

Consider the situation of the preaching minister who really wants God to have his best efforts. He is zealous for the cause of Christ and loves people. His sermons are inspiring and uplifting. He is popular in the community. What happens? Soon his popularity becomes a detriment to his preaching and teaching ministry. He is invited to participate in an endless round of community affairs. His counseling responsibilities increase daily. New members mean more visitation in the hospitals. The workload is soon beyond him. Criticism may follow his failure to keep up. His study and his health suffer.

The equipping ministry offers a whole new way of ministerial life. Those who are more experienced Christians are constantly guided into meaningful ministries. Because of their other occupations, most people in the pews cannot give eight hours a day in active Christian ministry. But they do have several free hours every week. Three or four hours multiplied by two hundred members provides a congregation with an additional six or eight hundred hours of ministry every week. Ideally then, an average-sized congregation, by developing its own ministry, can gain the equivalent of a dozen full-time paid staff members.

Think of the new opportunities the equipping concept offers the preaching minister. He no longer feels the psychological burden for every phase of activity in the church. The work is being done. The whole body is ministering to itself and to others. Lives are being touched everywhere. Meanwhile, his responsibility to "feed the flock" is not being neglected.

joy in the congregation

The practice of the equipping ministry makes it possible for a congregation to pulsate with new life. Because the members are participating in more than a pew-sitting/give-your-offering type of arrangement, they find new satisfaction in the service of Christ. They assume psychological ownership for the work of the church. It is now "my church" rather than "the minister and his church."

For a feeling of joy to continue, every member must have a sense of belonging to one another. They should not neglect meeting together, nor the ministry of encouraging one another (Hebrews 10:25). Genuine fellowship holds a vital place in today's church as it did among the early Christians (Acts 2:42).

Picture the difference in worship on Sunday morning. We now have a ministering congregation. During the week, some of the church leaders have been visiting the sick. Other families are sponsoring home Bible study groups. One man is leading in a food and clothing drive for a family whose home burned to the ground. A lady is there who has led a teenage girl to Christ during the past week. All of these worshipers carry in their hearts the warm glow of being Christ's ministers. They are finding exhilaration in life because of their selfless labors.

Furthermore, these families are not barred from participating in church life at the decision-making level.

They are not required to check their head along with their hat in the foyer. Every major part of congregational life is reviewed by as many people as possible. New programs are not handed down "from on high" by the preaching minister and a few of his cronies.

How could such an emphasis fail to produce a new sense of well-being in the congregation? Not only is it Biblical, this procedure follows sound psychological and sociological principles for healthy group response. Conducted in the right manner, the equipping ministry cannot fail.

Congregations assume a kind of corporate personality. Some churches are happy, and others are not. Some sing with enthusiasm, whereas others can scarcely be heard. Some churches are suspicious of newcomers, while others are immediately warm and receptive. What accounts for these differences? Many variables help produce these contrasting patterns of response. *The one constant determining factor, it seems, is the quality of participation by the people in the pews.*

liberation and responsibility

It is difficult for some preaching ministers to trust people in the pews with responsibility. Few seminary students even suspect that the average church member wants to become more involved in kingdom work. The experience of veteran preaching ministers, however, teaches that many people in the pew want to develop a personal ministry for which they are well-suited. They are willing, even eager, to do a job for the church when they are called to the task and trained to do it well.

Many preaching ministers will agree that the equipping-ministry principle is a good idea. Then they add,

"But it simply won't work." To bolster their position, they cite unsuccessful examples of giving responsibility to other members of the congregation. "I finally ended up doing it myself" is the usual rejoinder.

One cannot read the book of Acts carefully and fail to be impressed with the high quality of participation by the early Christians. It would have been impossible for the apostles alone to fill Jerusalem with the teachings of Jesus (Acts 5:28). Commenting on the spread of the gospel throughout the ancient world, Stephen Neill writes *"What is clear is that every Christian was a witness. Where there were Christians, there would be a living, burning faith, and before long, an expanding Christian community"* (italics mine).

Surely, it is not illusionary to believe that the average Christian today wants his life to count for Christ in a greater way. How else does one explain the Sunday-by-Sunday faithfulness of the people in the pews? Sometimes the pulpit fare has been woefully inadequate. Yet, the same people continue steadfastly in public worship. Many, like the Ethiopian who inquired about the way of salvation, are asking, "How?" "How can we be better Christians?" "How can we be better servants of Jesus Christ?"

The heart of the equipping ministry is a belief in the basic goodness of the majority of people in the congregation. To falter at this crucial level is to fail with the whole principle. We must give people a good name if they are to attain high ideals and practices. Otherwise, the venture into an equipping ministry ends in defeat.

Learning through new experiences takes a lifetime. Education has been called a controlled process of growth. Physical and spiritual growth both require time.

An equipping minister who is well acquainted with the congregation has knowledge about the gifts and capabilities of people. His task is to assist them in climbing the stairway of Christian responsibility. Together, they are both liberated to carry on their ministry for Christ.

the dangers of an equipping ministry

It is foolish to talk about the equipping ministry without discussing some of the pitfalls. Paul cautioned Timothy about hastiness when choosing new leadership (1 Timothy 5:22). He also spoke of those who have the desire "to be teachers of the law, without understanding either what they are saying or the things about which they make assertions" (1 Timothy 1:7). Phillips Brooks referred to the dangers of a "congregation in a congregation" composed of "half clergy half laymen."

Sometimes in a new congregation, a leadership vacuum develops. A well-meaning layman may step into a position of power. For the first time he is free to create policies and to determine the level of participation by others. Instead of practicing the equipping-ministry principle, he assumes the role of a dominating clergyman. He looks upon others in the congregation as potential threats to his power. He may even become competitive with a paid preaching minister when the congregation calls one. He can make life miserable for anyone who challenges his usurped authority.

Many preaching ministers have come to a new appreciation of Paul's warning to Timothy about untried leadership. The reference rings with relevancy when a congregation suffers due to misjudgments in recruitment. It is important to seek the right person at the right time for the right position. Otherwise, no one can function efficiently and happily.

Preaching ministers who are reluctant to trust ministers in the pews with responsibility should look more closely at their own profession. Many good churches have been torn apart by preachers who prove to be fierce wolves among the flock (Acts 20:29). Or to use another figure, sometimes all a congregation can do is wait for the storm caused by a preaching minister to subside. The only optimism about a hurricane is that, eventually, it blows itself out.

It is always risky to train leadership in the church. Jesus himself admitted He had chosen one who was a devil (John 6:70). The church, however, does not give up the idea of equipping others for leadership simply because some abuse their position. A far greater tragedy is to neglect those tens of thousands who have high potential for kingdom service.

Those who minister for Christ today owe their function in the church to someone else who helped prepare them for leadership. The present generation must have faith in future workers. Otherwise, they are betraying the trust given to themselves. The apostle Paul helped to equip Timothy for ministry. He instructed him, however, to keep passing along what he had learned: "And what you have heard from me before many witnesses entrust to faithful men who will be able to teach others also" (2 Timothy 2:2). Part of the responsibility of each generation of Christians is to prepare leadership for the next.

A PRACTICAL APPLICATION
OF THE PRINCIPLE

what practical change?

What practical difference will the equipping ministry make in the life of the church? In other words, what is the basic value of the principle? We must constantly guard against those inert ideas which lead us nowhere. Christianity always makes a difference in individuals and societies wherever it is preached and practiced.

The equipping ministry should enable a church to attain a higher quality of life because it taps the latent energies within a congregation. Once these resources become available to enough churches, a spiritual explosion could rock the world.

Church history is a panorama of change and adjustment in the life of the church. Often a chosen route led to disastrous consequences for the spread of the gospel. The New Testament, like a ship's compass, has helped the church regain its course again and again. And each time these changes have been made, the church makes progress on her pilgrimage.

changes in worship

Assuming a congregation adopts the principle of the equipping ministry, what changes in worship could we envision? Sunday morning worship time for many churches has become a rather humdrum experience. Many members carefully watch the clock. Sleeping officers are not unheard of.

Previously pointed out was the fact that repeated worship services *without participation by the members* can desensitize the emotions. When Luke tells us the early Christians were "devoted" to the apostle's teaching and to fellowship, he uses a Greek word which conveys the idea of intensity. Those early Christians were evidently excited about their worship.

Once we acknowledge that the congregation is composed of Christ's ministers, then the weekly worship time becomes a meeting of the "ministerial association." Such an experience will provide inspiration, instruction, and fellowship for the "ministers." Those who attend are not simply putting in their time. They are finding assistance for their personal ministries.

The worship service should be much more than just a good habit. Every song should have a definite purpose. Every Scripture should be chosen from a particular point of view. The focus, of course, must be upon God, but the question still remains, "How can each worshiper function best as Christ's minister?"

In a free church tradition, a committee can look over the Christian year and make suggestions to the congregation. For example, God's ministers need a devout prayer life. Several services can be devoted to this topic. God's ministers must be forgiving. Again, follow the same procedure. With this method, a whole congregation can be lifted to a higher level of participation and concern. We must not emphasize individual spiritual growth to the exclusion of emphasis upon corporate growth.

changes in sermonizing

Surveys on church attendance in America indicate the high priority which Americans place on the sermon.

Every preaching minister in America, then, should be sensitive to the importance of his work in the pulpit.

What is the purpose of the sermon in the context of the equipping ministry? Surely the objective must be more than simply the euphoric feeling which accompanies spellbinding oratory. The sermon, of course, should have emotional power. Richard Baxter cried out in the seventeenth century to a lethargic clergy, "What! Speak coldly for God and for men's salvation? Can we believe that our people must be converted or condemned and yet we speak in a drowsy tone? In the name of God, brethren, labor to awaken your heart before you get to the pulpit."

Unfortunately perhaps, in the history of the church the chaplets of honor have frequently been placed upon the heads of the preaching giants. The accolades have been heaped upon the spellbinder rather than upon the more average servant of the Lord Jesus.

To add such a note is not intended in any way to detract from men whose gifts in the pulpit exceed those of the average preacher. It is to say, however, that greater influence for the kingdom may come, in the long run, through the efforts of a hard-working pastor-teacher who across the years has patiently prepared hundreds of others to minister.

Few ministers are capable of eloquent oratory Sunday after Sunday. The equipping ministry removes the burden of that unwritten expectation. Equipping ministers see their sermonizing over the years as the patient and prayerful preparation of others to minister. On some Sundays, his preaching may shine and the congregation will be especially edified. At other times, when he is not satisfied with his efforts, he need not feel he has failed.

He may have sown the seed that simply needs more time to germinate and blossom.

Successful preaching is not necessarily indicated by large attendance figures. Nor is the acid test of good preaching the number of "amens" which the sermon elicits. The real proof is the increasing number of Christians who are involved in ministry. Let the "amens" come, of course, and thank God for them. Just remember that preaching is judged to be "good" and "successful" by different criteria in the equipping ministry.

As Karl Barth reminds us, the burden of speech in the Christian community is not just "knowledge," but "active knowledge." Speech must never be minimized since it precedes knowledge. Yet our knowledge without action is a means without an end.

The true objective of every sermon is determined when the speaker answers the question, "Just what do I intend for people to do as a result of this message?" Unless the speaker himself has an idea of some concrete response, how is it possible for the hearers to know what is expected of them?

changes in study

The idea of study in the Christian community has been present since the beginnings of Christianity. The priority given to learning in Judaism made it very natural for Christians to continue the same emphasis. Proverbs is filled with elation about "wisdom." The gain of wisdom is far better than silver or gold (Proverbs 3:14). In the New Testament we learn that Jesus himself increased in wisdom (Luke 2:52), and Timothy is admonished to "continue in what you have learned and have firmly believed" (2 Timothy 3:14).

Throughout her history, the church has expressed her interest in study through various types of schools. The catechetical school, the cathedral school, the parochial school, and the Sunday school are examples of the concern of the church for learning and knowledge. One of the largest study movements in recent centuries has been the Sunday school with its strong emphasis upon lay participation.

The adoption of the Uniform Lessons (the study of the same portion of Scripture by many religious groups on a particular Sunday) provides an effective system for improving Bible knowledge. Millions of Americans have gained a panoramic view of the Bible through this method.

Thousands of Sunday-school classes have been started across the nation where members come to study. Frequently, however, little attention is given to the idea of training more ministers for service in the kingdom. *The whole process often becomes study for the sake of study rather than study for the sake of ministry.* The writer of Hebrews was distressed because those who had been taught were not prepared to teach others (Hebrews 5:12). The recipients of the letter had evidently missed the whole point of his teaching because they were not actively engaged in ministry themselves. Instead, they needed to be taught first principles again.

How does the equipping ministry change the usual emphasis of the modern Sunday school? Certainly, it in no way minimizes the need for Christians to have the Word of God in their hearts and lives (Proverbs 4:21). Nor does it overlook the Bible as the Christian sourcebook of truth and knowledge. Every healthy congregation must be nourished by Bible teaching. At the same time, the Sunday school must also teach people how to channel their knowledge into Christian activity. The scribes and Pharisees in the New Testament were excellent students of the Scriptures, but they had evidently missed the point of active, compassionate service for others.

A number of churches, recognizing the disparity between content and action in the average Sunday school, are supplementing their study programs with training centers or "mini-colleges." Although these centers include study, they are primarily geared for action.

Sunday school too can become more action-oriented. Courses can be taught on a variety of ministries in the life of the church. Classes on teaching, shepherding, calling, new-church planting, counseling, family witnessing, preaching, and music participation could all be offered during the time for Sunday school. These courses would each include on-the-field training as well as participation in class. The class on preaching, for example, should include a sermon brought to the class by each member.

A class on calling could be scheduled on Saturday morning from 9:00 a.m. to 12:00 noon. Many religious groups are discovering this time as the best opportunity to visit for Christ in the community. People are usually home during these hours. Also, calling during the day helps to eliminate some of the fear factor in night-time visitation.

The following schedule may be followed or adapted:

9:00 - 9:45	Instruction and Prayer
9:45 - 10:00	Assignments Given/Teams Chosen
10:00 - 12:00	Calling
12:00 - 1:00	Light Lunch and Report Session

This arrangement has been implemented in various cities across the nation. The results have been very satisfactory. Contrary to popular belief, Americans who are approached by concerned members of a congregation are usually not resentful. A new light comes into the eyes of hundreds of Christians who find the courage for the first time to approach another human being on behalf of Christ. The report session during the lunch hour is usually a time of joy and gladness.

The possibilities of evening calling in many communities is still not to be ruled out. Sometimes hours after dark are the only ones available. Appointment calling and home Bible-study sessions are especially feasible at night.

other changes

Not only will the average congregation be changed in its study and preaching program through the equipping ministry; other areas will be influenced as well. For example, laymen can participate more effectively in worship. In many churches, the preaching minister conducts almost the entire worship service by himself. Why not entrust ministers in the pews with a much greater portion of the time for public worship, and on various occasions, with the preaching itself? In addition to the worship experience, every Sunday offers a living testimony to the ministry of all believers.

Other changes need to take place in the area of social service. The congregation should be an important part of community life. By participating in schools, hospitals, clubs, parks, city government, and other area interests, Christians can demonstrate their concern for the quality of life here and now.

It is possible for a congregation to ask a member to be a "minister" with a particular institution. These ministers could bring periodic reports to the congregation regarding the area of their service. Many times, responsibilities in public service are carried by the preaching minister until he is exhausted from his participation in community affairs. Why not pass along these responsibilities to others? A retiree, for example, may find new zest for living through a ministry in the hospital or a nursing home.

According to the New Testament, women were given a high place in the first-century church. Peter heralds a new day in the kingdom by announcing "your sons *and your daughters* shall prophesy" (Acts 2:17). Paul speaks gratefully of Euodia and Syntyche, two women in Philippi who, he says, "labored side by side with me in the gospel together with Clement and the rest of my fellow workers" (Philippians 4:2, 3). Priscilla joins with her husband in expounding "the way of God more accurately" to Apollos (Acts 18:26).

Two Pauline passages of Scripture have created problems regarding the participation of women in the life and work of the church. In his Corinthian correspondence, Paul mentions the disturbances taking place in public worship. Evidently, women were a part of the problem. He therefore told the women *in this situation* to "keep silence in the churches" (1 Corinthians 14:34). A similar reference is in the letters to Timothy. Here the passage reads, "I permit no woman to teach or to have authority over men; she is to keep silent" (1 Timothy 2:12).

It is faulty exegesis to take a "particular" in the Scripture and elevate it to a "universal." In both of these passages, the apostle is dealing with a particular problem. In the first, women were creating disturbances. In the second, they were evidently usurping authority in the congregation. In both situations, they are told to be silent. For the same instruction to apply today, we must have a similar situation. Otherwise the strong ministry of women throughout the New Testament, obviously with apostolic approval, is inconsistent.

Women will find an expression for their gifts and abilities. If they are denied the opportunity to use them through the church, then they will find other interests. It is a tragedy for women to be without a place to serve in many churches when they have such an important contribution to make. What better way could the equipping-ministry ideal be expressed than to include the half of the human race so frequently neglected in the life of the church?

EQUIPPING OTHERS FOR MINISTRY

the importance of personal preparation

The preaching minister who adopts the equipping ministry needs to realize he is operating on an entirely different principle than the one-person-clergy concept. It is extremely important for him to have a clear understanding of his own role.

He must seek constantly to eliminate obligations on the periphery of his central task. A thousand duties will come along begging for his attention. He must decide which responsibilities are directly his and which ones can be successfully delegated to others.

No passage of Scripture is more instructive at this point than the incident in Jerusalem regarding the Grecian widows (Acts 6:1-7). Here we have a troublesome situation which could have eventually stopped the spread of the gospel. It was emotionally charged with racial overtones. All the energies of the apostles might have been absorbed by it. The apostles easily could have stepped in and tried to administer the program of benevolence by themselves. Instead they said, "Pick out from among you seven men of good repute, full of the Spirit and of wisdom, whom we may appoint to this duty. But we will devote ourselves to prayer and to the ministry of the word" (Acts 6:3, 4). The apostles refused to be turned aside from their primary task of prayer and preaching.

The equipping ministry continually prepares others for the work to be done. The preaching minister needs an overview of the total ministry of the congregation, not only the tasks to be accomplished, but also the resources of those willing to help. This overview can be gained best by relying on wise counselors in the church. These counselors may be among those in the congregation who are also helping to equip others.

Once the preaching minister, through prayer and consultation, has a fairly clear picture of what needs to be accomplished, he should put into motion the means to carry out the task. A warning is in order here. He must be careful not to place himself in the position of bending the wills of others to suit his own. Otherwise, he may be guilty of violating the sacredness of human personality. Church members are not pawns on some kind of ecclesiastical chessboard to be moved around at will.

Preaching ministers and those in political life face similar temptations. They may want to surround themselves with "yes" men in order to avoid any possible confrontation. This natural inclination may be fatal to creative leadership. Everyone knows the story of Lincoln, the President, and Stanton, the Secretary of War. Stanton sharply criticized Lincoln constantly. When Lincoln was asked why he retained Stanton in his cabinet, he replied simply: "He's the best man for the job."

When a minister has been with a congregation long enough to consolidate his reserves of power, he may be tempted to unseat all those who disagree with his policies. It is true, of course, that the work of Christ cannot go forward in the midst of bitter strife and wrangling. He may feel justified, therefore, in seeing his "opponent" removed from a position of authority. Taking such a drastic measure, however, may deprive him of a counselor who is brave enough to point out his faults.

A business leader said on one occasion, "If you want to be successful in life, find a good critic. Listen to what he says about your faults. If he is on target, change your ways. If he is not, forget it. Then, one day, when you are on your way in leadership, write him a letter and thank him for helping you."

The preaching minister prepares himself by always being aware of his responsibility to others. Jesus said regarding His disciples, "For their sake I consecrate myself, that they also may be consecrated in truth" (John 17:19). Here is one key to the door of a successful equipping ministry. Because he is constantly aware of the influence of his life upon others, the preaching minister reconsecrates himself daily to the task.

living stones

In Peter's first epistle in the New Testament is painted a picture of Christians forming a spiritual cathedral. The author writes, "And like living stones be yourselves built into a spiritual house, to be a holy priesthood, to offer spiritual sacrifices acceptable to God through Jesus Christ" (1 Peter 2:5).

Where in the New Testament do we find a better picture of every Christian functioning as a minister before God? In fact, Peter does not hesitate to use the word *priesthood*, and sees every believer functioning as one of God's priests. Very clearly stated is the important doctrine of the priesthood of all believers. This doctrine, recovered in theory during the Reformation, never has been recovered fully in practice, even in our present time.

Suppose an equipping minister is called to serve in a one-man-minister situation. What does he do? Where does he begin? It is important to give people enough background in this concept before trying to implement it. Careful groundwork needs to be laid, both from the pulpit and in the classroom. Without a carefully laid instructional foundation, the preaching minister may build a straw house.

People do not identify closely with those institutions where they are denied psychological ownership. Here is the important key: "belonging." Sociology teaches us about primary and secondary relationships. The human family is one example of a primary relationship. The church will never become a "family" unless the members are actively participating in her ministry. Those with gifts of leadership, who are denied the opportunity to exercise their abilities, will simply find other outlets for their energies. We sometimes forget the voluntary nature of the church as a social institution.

Many preaching ministers are afraid to pass along genuine responsibilities to others. They may feel a task will not be carried out to the level of their own expectations. They may have experienced the frustration of delegating a responsibility to someone else who did nothing about it. Giving the job to another member might have caused hard feelings.

The price of progress sometimes includes seeing the work being handled in a very immature way. No professional, however, attains to high proficiency on the first few tries. Continued practice is required for skill development. To deny others the chance to practice is to deny them the opportunity of becoming an efficient worker for Jesus Christ.

Some leaders in the church see the church program as a kind of "blue plate special" at the local truck stop. Everyone who comes is limited to the same menu. Ideally, the church is more like a cafeteria. No one is re-

quired to eat everything along the line. People have vary-
ing spiritual needs. Some require more nourishment than
others. Some may be receiving fellowship and teaching
outside the local church. A wise spiritual chef plans the
menu to fit the different needs of individuals.

To use another illustration, no college expects the
seniors to sit through freshman orientation year after
year. The upperclassmen are expected to advance to
more difficult subjects. Furthermore, they are not be-
rated for failing to enroll in orientation. Each part of the
curriculum is designed to move the students on to the
next level. Putting students through the same learning
experiences year after year is to invite boredom and
intellectual laziness. Paul does not commend the Corinthians for needing more milk. He reproves them (1 Corinthians 3:2).

Much has been said about the average congregation
being too busy to evangelize. It is not wise to plan
church activities every night of the week *if the same
people are expected to attend every session*. The preaching minister and his family should not be required to be
present every time the church doors are open. Like other
members of the congregation, they need some time together at home. The high spiritual casualty rate of the
children of preaching ministers can be partially attrib-
uted to unwise planning of church calendars.

The calendar followed by the congregation needs to
be planned with care. It should include a variety
of growing and learning experiences for members and
nonmembers. All age groups at every level of spiritual
discernment need to be considered. Then each group,
after being apprised of their spiritual opportunities, can
enjoy participation. Unless members can willingly and

openly respond to the services being offered them, how can the spirit of gladness ring throughout the church? A service filled with duty-oriented clock-watchers is devoid of any joy.

recognizing gifts in the church

Part of the continuing ministry of the ascended Christ is to impart gifts to His body, the church. The exalted Lord through His Spirit bestows "presents" upon His church (1 Corinthians 12:1-11; Ephesians 4:9-11). These gifts have a variety and yet a oneness about them. The variety stems from their difference in the kinds received. Their oneness stems from the one Lord and the one Spirit who gives them.

One purpose of Christian gifts is "for building up the body of Christ" (Ephesians 4:12). Jesus provides them for His church in order to help stimulate growth. They are given for the good of the entire body and must not be used in a selfish or a disruptive way. Love must always govern their expression (1 Corinthians 12:31—13:13).

Gifts within the church are both independent and interdependent. Using the illustration of the human body, Paul reminded the Corinthians of the interdependence of the various parts. He pointed out the absurdity of the eye saying to the hand, "I have no need of you" and the head which announces its independence from the feet (1 Corinthians 12:12-26).

Even though the gifts to the body are distributed to individuals, they each have a mutuality about them. I am allowed to practice my gifts in the context of allowing others the same privilege. If I deny others their right, I am violating the whole concept of the body with particular members responsible for special functions.

The subject of gifts has greater significance when considered in the context of the ministry of all believers. What need is there to talk about discovering the gifts of others if the church is simply the stage for the preaching minister's abilities? Even though a congregation may be filled with "gifts," the one-man-ministry system allows little opportunity for their exercise.

Now that a new emphasis is being placed upon the ministry of every Christian, the importance of individuals discovering their gifts is underscored. Here is the way the body builds itself up. By discovering the "presents" each has received, the whole body grows. Paul saw in Timothy the gifts of preaching and teaching and did not hesitate to recruit him for public service (Acts 16:1-5).

A wise equipping minister will recognize within the congregation dozens of latent gifts. In some cases, the gifted person may be unaware of his abilities. Such gifts need only development and exercise in order to be a great blessing to the family of God. The one who is encouraged to use his ability finds joy and satisfaction in its expression.

On the other hand, the church may need to offer help to someone who is mistaken about his "gift." A member with wonderful abilities in one kind of ministry may be a failure in another. It takes courage to tell someone gently that he has appraised his gifts inaccurately.

exercise through study and practices

Paul is not hesitant to tell Timothy, "Do not neglect the gift you have" (1 Timothy 4:14). With the exception of a few religious groups, it has become the accepted practice to send young men with abilities in preaching to schools of the ministry. What the church has been faithful to exercise in regard to the ministry from the pulpit, however, it has woefully neglected for its ministry from the pew.

The appendix of this study offers a list of suggested courses which could be offered by a congregation or by a cluster of churches in an area. These courses are designed to help members discover their particular gifts and to exercise them. They are not the product of theoretical research. They come out of actual training situations where they have been taught.

Look at these courses very carefully. Then, think about how they could be offered in your own community. Just as a new college may not be able to complete its faculty and curriculum during the first semester, you may need to allow time for your "school of the ministry" to grow. Caution: unless those who enroll in action-type courses are given on-the-job training, much of the basic learning experience will be lost.

For example, a class in "shepherding" could be offered. Members of the congregation with pastoral gifts need help in developing those gifts. Here is the opportunity for the preaching minister to take someone with him during his pastoral visits. While he is making calls on the elderly, the shut-ins, and those who are ill, he can be instructing someone else.

One preaching minister usually asks someone else to sit in on his counseling sessions. He explains to the counselee that the extra person is an intern in the counseling ministry of the church. He asks for permission for him to stay. In almost every instance, the one being counseled offers no objections. Obviously, such trainees must be mature, discreet, and respected. Prospects for this type of equipping may be few.

When I was a boy, my father took me with him to make evangelistic calls. This practice proved during the early years of my own ministry to be a very important dimension of my training. The preaching minister who takes others with him on his outreach calls helps a congregation gain strength in leadership. His influence will continue to profit the congregation, even after he is gone.

No principle or idea, no matter how sound, will have any lasting impression unless it is put into operation. The congregation that "practices" equipping ministry, as well as "thinks" it, has every possibility of becoming a powerful influence for Christ in the community.

HOPE FOR EVANGELIZATION

in this generation

The Biblical concept of the equipping ministry offers the only real hope for world evangelization by this generation. The Great Commission of Jesus constitutes the evangelistic charter of the Christian church. We can stop speaking about "church growth" only when that commission is fulfilled. Jesus realized He was giving His disciples a superhuman task. He therefore promised them superhuman authority and power (Matthew 28:18-20).

From the early days of the church, Christians have dreamed of carrying out the Commission in their own generation. The apostle Paul was not content with his evangelistic labors, even after he had preached the gospel in many of the metropolitan centers of the ancient world. He still yearned to go on to Spain (Romans 15:24, 28). In the evangelistic enterprise, "a man's reach should exceed his grasp," until the world has been successfully evangelized.

Comparatively speaking, Christianity has been a phenomenal success. More people reverence the name of Jesus Christ than any other. Christianity in all its forms counts nearly a billion followers. No other religion in the history of civilization can claim such victories.

That is the good news. The bad news is that an estimated three billion people on this globe have never heard the claims of Christ in a face-to-face situation. We should be weeping daily for those who even now have never had the opportunity to know Christ.

America herself is a great mission field. About three out of every four homes in America are not actively involved with any congregation. Forty-five million children are not a part of any Sunday school. Approximately one-fourth of the nation's population live in the great megalopolis which extends from Washington, D.C. to Boston. Here is one continuous strip city, 450 miles long and one hundred miles wide. It is one of many great missionary opportunities.

What then should be our goal and what are the means of attaining it? *Our goal must be world evangelization during our own generation.* We will not be held accountable for past generations nor for the generations of the future. We are responsible, however, for our own time. It is traitorous to Jesus Christ, our commander-in-chief, to accept any goal less than the one He gave to the church. As one missionary reminds us, "Some people do not believe in missions. They have no right to believe in missions; they do not believe in Christ."

impossibility under current circumstances

The vision of evangelizing the world in this generation is not hopeful in view of current attitudes in the church regarding the ministry. The average American congregation is not evangelistic, even in its own community. Little wonder then that the concern for world evangelization is minimal.

In the American situation, the preaching minister is usually so occupied with pastoral responsibilities he has little time left to think about outreach. Since the prospect of calling in strange homes may arouse fears of personal rejection, he tends to find other outlets for his spiritual concerns.

The goal of presenting the gospel to every home in America demands a better performance record on the part of American churches. At the present level of evangelistic achievements, even the goal of evangelizing the United States is unattainable. Most American congregations seem dedicated to *status quo* rather than committed to a systematic program of community outreach and growth.

We sometimes praise the American churches for being good. They are good. But the majority of Americans will die in their sins unless churches change radically. No halfway measures are sufficient to meet the needs of the times. No less than a complete about-face in thinking and practice and dedication can make possible the fulfillment of Christ's command.

The scope of the Great Commission has always been "the world." Some parts of the globe today are sealed off politically from the Christian evangel. In the providence of God, however, closed countries sometimes become open ones. Unforeseen political upheavals have often changed the whole national climate with favorable implications for the presentation of the gospel.

The church must always be prepared and ready to enter a closed country. At the same time, millions of dollars and equipping ministers by the tens of thousands should be poured into those countries where the door is open. Thousands of healthy, growing congregations, indigenous to the country and place, must always be our primary goal.

the dream of an immense task force

With all the failings of American Christianity, this country still has one of the highest ratios of church attendance to population of any nation in the world. In spite of the entrenched forces of wickedness, the spiritual roots in America go very deep. In contrast, the beautiful cathedrals in Europe are practically empty on Sunday morning.

Some of the American religious groups have doctrines which place them on the fringes of historic Biblical Christianity. At the same time, encouraging changes are being made in unlikely places. Renewed interest in Bible study today is leading many groups toward New Testament doctrines and practices.

The greatest day for the gospel may lie just around the corner. The future offers a magnificent opportunity to find millions who are ready to reject human idols for the living God.

If equipping ministries are initiated in thousands of American churches, it will unleash one of the mightiest task forces in the history of the universe. World Wars I and II pressed millions of men into the service of our country in only a matter of months.

Just suppose millions of ministers in the pew were equipped and trained for Christian service. Thousands of congregations would begin to put into operation a plan to release the latent energies of the church. Ministers in the pulpit could devote more of their time to the preaching of the Word. Followers of Christ would look for places of service not only in this country but around the world. Such an operation could be the mightiest in history. Furthermore, it would be backed by the superhuman authority of Jesus himself who has promised His continued presence.

During the past two decades, Americans have been pouring nearly a billion dollars every year into the construction of new church buildings. Such giving power presents almost unlimited financial resources for world evangelism. Christians have dreamed for centuries of the "world hearing his voice." It is well within the range of possibility for that dream to come true in our generation.

social and political impact

The most powerful social and political force in the world is the church. Man-made laws change with the flux of opinion and power structures. Even the decisions of our Supreme Court change with the climate of the American opinion. The gospel offers the necessary absolutes on which to build lasting human relationships. Dreams for a perfect society, however, will never be fulfilled in America or any other country. The claims of the gospel will always be rejected by some, even among those in the churches. As long as the hearts of people are unconverted, social disorder will prevail. As Nicholas Berdyaev, the philosopher, reminds us, "the sinfulness of human nature does not mean that social improvements are impossible but that a perfect and absolute social order" can never exist.

Even though a perfect society will always be beyond our grasp, the "salt and light" principle in the Sermon on the Mount still holds true. The influence of the gospel in our world is simply immeasurable. Consider for a moment the effect upon American society if the influence of the church were to be suddenly withdrawn.

Changes in a society take place when a sufficient number of people have a change of heart which produces a change of life. In the Biblical sense, they are "converted" or "born again." True converts will reproduce themselves many times over. As the society is permeated with the spirit of Christ, the social consequences which follow tend to make it easier for other individuals to follow Christ.

An aggressive movement of the American churches in a concern-for-people type of evangelism could bring changes in the social and political life of America scarcely imagined. The church can move in a sphere where the government is almost completely helpless. Laws do not necessarily change attitudes. The conversion of millions of Americans to Christ through the preaching and teaching of the gospel offers this nation's best hope. Far from the stance of "civil religion," this view simply reflects the Biblical admonition, "Righteousness exalts a nation, but sin is a reproach to any people" (Proverbs 14:34).

conclusion

Church growth viewed as a continuing onward and upward pattern is a delusion. Every experienced Christian leader knows the variables of human personality. The progress of the church in evangelism can best be charted, not by a constant upward line, but by graphing peaks and valleys like a mountainous terrain.

The apostle Paul was certainly aware of the recurring danger of setbacks for the progress of the gospel. He warned Timothy about losses in evangelism by reminding him of what happened in Asia. "You are aware that all who are in Asia turned away from me," he said, "and among them Phygelus and Hermogenes" (2 Timothy 1:15).

Patience and steadfastness have always been important twin concepts in church growth. Rather than giving his body in one flaming burnt offering, the minister for

Christ offers his life as a "living sacrifice." His body is consumed by toil and service for Christ day after day. Through the minister's devotional life, his faith and resolve are rekindled for the on-going task.

We may never know where our greatest victories lie. An out-of-the-way village church may be actually the vanguard for future action. Nowhere in the New Testament is the servant of Jesus Christ judged by his numerical successes, but everywhere in terms of his faithfulness. Sometimes, what seems to be our blackest failure may prove to be our greatest victory.

When dark days come, as they surely will, then the minister of Christ must hold firm to his convictions. For surely as the sunrise, "the kingdom of the world" will indeed, "become the kingdom of our Lord and of his Christ" (Revelation 11:15).

As the American poet, Vachel Lindsay, has so wonderfully expressed in his gem, "Foreign Missions in Battle Array":

> This is our faith tremendous,
>   Our wild hope, who shall scorn,
> That in the name of Jesus
>   The world shall be reborn!

APPENDIX:

SUGGESTED COURSE OFFERINGS

REFERENCES AND COMMENTS

**THE AMERICAN CHURCH GROWTH
STUDY SERIES**

**STEPS TO USING
THE AMERICAN CHURCH GROWTH
STUDY SERIES**

**RESOURCES FOR AMERICAN
CHURCH GROWTH**

SUGGESTED COURSE OFFERINGS

church growth

101 BASIC PRINCIPLES OF CHURCH GROWTH

An examination of the New Testament teaching on the growth and expansion of the church. Special attention will be given to the Biblical concept of the ministry of all believers.

102 CALLING FOR CHRIST

An action-oriented class where members are not only provided instruction, but actual on-the-field experience in survey work and witnessing for Christ.

103 THE HOUSE CHURCH

A study of the house churches in the New Testament and the possibilities which they offer for world evangelism. Procedures and methods for organizing a house church will be given. Special attention will be given to the house church in the new community.

104 NEW CHURCH PLANTING

What is the best way for a church to mother a new congregation? How can some of the difficulties which so often beset new churches be avoided? What is the relationship between new churches and church growth? These questions and others will be handled in this course.

105 MISSIONARY PROGRAMMING

A careful study of the best way to develop a strong

missions strategy by the local congregation. Emphasis will be placed on program and personnel.

106 LIFESTYLE EVANGELISM
Sometimes referred to as "spontaneous evangelism," or "friendship evangelism," this study suggests ways for Christians to interact positively with those whom they meet, or are associated with, in the everyday walk of life.

107 COMMUNICATING CHRIST IN OUR CULTURE
A pre-evangelism course designed to acquaint Christians with the thought patterns of non-Christians. Why do people reject the gospel? What are some of the basic barriers to belief? Designed to equip Christians to help the lost find their way to Christ.

public speaking

110 DESIGNING THE SERMON
A fundamental course for the person in the pew who wants to learn some basic principles for communication from the pulpit.

111 EXPOSITORY PREACHING
A course for the person who has already succeeded in doing a limited amount of preaching, but who wants to learn more about utilizing the Bible for preaching.

112 HOW TO SPEAK IN PUBLIC
A course designed to aid the Christian leader in

speech preparation and delivery. Special attention will be given to such subjects as how to introduce a speaker, acting as master of ceremonies, presenting an award, accepting an office, preparing and presenting a devotional, and leading a discussion.

counseling and shepherding

120 PRINCIPLES OF PSYCHOLOGY

Designed to acquaint the student with important facts relating to behavior and mental life. Especially helpful to those who minister on a person-to-person basis with people.

121 COUNSELING

For the person who wants to gain basic insights into areas of counseling. Formal types of counseling as well as "sidewalk" counseling will be considered.

122 SHEPHERDING THE FLOCK

A careful study of the problems and methods in conducting a shepherding plan that involves many Christians in an effective ministry to sick, infirmed, troubled, bereaved, and inactive members.

123 HOSPITAL VISITATION

Those who are ill often need special attention and care from other Christians. It is frequently a time of personal self-examination. Members of the congregation who visit others in the hospital will especially benefit from this course.

christian education

130 TEACHING

The purpose of this class is to help develop good teachers. Class members will be learning age characteristics, how to compose a lesson, how to communicate effectively, how to challenge pupils, and many other characteristics of good teaching. A refresher course for those already teaching as well as for potential new teachers.

131 TEACHING THE BIBLE TO CHILDREN

Especially for teachers who are working with young people below the seventh grade in public school. A valuable course also for those who are interested in learning how to teach this age group. Learning experiences in the home will be considered.

132 WORKING WITH YOUTH

For those who are working with youth above the seventh grade in public schools. Emphasis will be upon young people learning to serve instead of being served. Also open to those who are interested in beginning a work with youth.

133 TEACHING ADULTS

Techniques for sparking interest in adult classes in the congregation. Emphasis will be placed upon the adult class as a source for additional teachers in a growing Sunday school.

143 HOME BIBLE STUDIES

An investigation of the home as a strategic place

for Christian witness. Consideration will be given to the starting of home Bible study groups, their development and outreach, as well as principles of leadership.

135 CAMPUS MINISTRY

A study of specialized ministry on the college and university campus. Open to those who are particularly interested in this important phase of Christian ministry.

music and public worship

140 PUBLIC WORSHIP

A study of the various ways to enrich and deepen the public worship. Especially helpful for those working with music or serving on worship committees.

141 BASIC SONG LEADING

Basic patterns of song leading. Includes actual practice in leading singing with the group. Also, the importance and value of hymn selection.

biblical

150 PERSONAL BIBLE STUDY

Helping an individual get the Bible into his mind and heart through his own personal study. Principles for understanding the Bible are included along with suggestions for meaningful reading.

151 DISCOVERING MY GIFTS

Utilizing the Bible as a sourcebook to help determine where each person can best make a contribution to the kingdom of God. Very useful to those who want to serve Christ in a larger way. Helps answer the questions "how" and "where"?

152 GREAT THEMES IN THE OLD TESTAMENT

An overview of basic Old Testament themes. A course basically designed for those who want a more comprehensive knowledge of the Old Testament.

153 INTRODUCTION TO THE NEW TESTAMENT

A basic introductory study of the New Testament with a general view of its origin and structure.

154 GREAT THEMES IN THE NEW TESTAMENT

An overview of basic New Testament themes. A course basically designed for those who want a more comprehensive knowledge of the New Testament.

155 THE BIBLE BOOK

A course on one of the books of the Bible, giving an overview and investigation of the content on a section-by-section basis. This course is further designed to assist students in making a study of the Bible by themselves.

156 BIBLICAL ARCHEOLOGY

A study of the relationship between Biblical study and archeology. Especially helpful for those who plan to visit the lands of the Bible.

personal growth

160 DEVOTIONAL LIFE

With the push-pull of modern society, how does a Christian develop and maintain a deepening devotional life?

161 CHRISTIAN RELATIONSHIPS

This course stresses the importance of positive family relationships, and the development of Christian attitudes toward neighbors and acquaintances.

163 FACING TEMPTATION

Sometimes the temptations of the world are almost overpowering. How does a Christian meet temptation and develop spiritually through the experience?

REFERENCES AND COMMENTS

INTRODUCTION

Neither the emphasis upon the ministry of all believers nor upon an equipping ministry is new in church history. One of the salient doctrines of the Reformation was the priesthood of all believers. The Pietistic movement in Germany and the Restoration movement in America carried with them a great concern for the participation of all Christians in ministry.

Unfortunately, it is much easier to recover a Biblical doctrine in theory than in practice. The congregation which puts this concept into practice is still a rarity. Suspicion and turmoil often arise in the church where an equipping preaching ministry is being introduced.

Some want to push the concept of an equipping ministry to the extreme of abolishing a paid "professional" ministry. I am wholeheartedly against such a move. The New Testament is very clear at this point.

In his Corinthian correspondence, Paul states his specific reasons for not taking financial remuneration from Corinth. He makes very definite, though, his God-given right to do so. Chapters eight and nine of both letters are devoted to a discussion of the Christian and giving. In a key verse, after he has reflected upon the practices of the Old Testament, he states, "In the same way, the Lord commanded that those who proclaim the gospel should get their living by the gospel" (1 Corinthians 9:14).

Paul later admits his mistake in not requiring financial support from the Corinthians. He even apologizes! He writes, "For in what were you less favored than the rest of the churches, except that I myself did not burden you?

Forgive me this wrong!" (2 Corinthians 12:13). Also, the elders, "who labor in preaching and teaching," he says, are worthy of "double honor" (1 Timothy 5:17). The "double honor" is clearly financial remuneration for their services.

From a practical point of view, the minister who has all his time to devote to preaching the gospel is freer to serve than someone who must earn his livelihood outside the church. Just as the American army will always need the help of graduates from West Point, the church can be benefited by a "professional" ministry. The crux of the issue is not whether a paid ministry is Biblically valid, but rather, how does a congregation best utilize the talents and abilities of those who have chosen church leadership as a career?

CHAPTER 1/UNDERSTANDING THE EQUIPPING MINISTRY

In addition to a restudy of the New Testament, one of the best ways to grasp the basic idea of the equipping ministry is to work through the "laity literature" which followed World War II. A THEOLOGY OF THE LAITY by Hendrik Kraemer (Westminster/1958) is a tremendously important study. Even more comprehensive is LAY PEOPLE IN THE CHURCH by Yves Congar (English edition/ Bloomsbury/1957).

D. Elton Trueblood may very well be the American scholar who has done the most to promote acceptance of the equipping-ministry concept in the United States during this era. His long list of fine titles (all by Harper) include YOUR OTHER VOCATION (1952), THE COMPANY OF THE COMMITTED (1961), and THE INCENDIARY FELLOWSHIP (1967).

For an incisive study of the equipping ministry of Jesus, I do not believe Robert E. Coleman's *THE MASTER PLAN OF EVANGELISM* (Revell/1963) has been surpassed. Marcus Barth deals extensively with what he calls Paul's *locus classicus* in Ephesians 4:11-13, *ANCHOR BIBLE* (Doubleday/1974). The student who is serious about the nature of ministry in the New Testament should not miss this discussion. Another very useful Biblical study is by Michael Green entitled *CALLED TO SERVE* (Westminister/1964).

I deeply regret the omission of Old Testament backgrounds for this book. The instruction of Jethro to Moses could be expanded into a very fruitful discussion (Exodus 18). The prophets abound with useful illustrations. This area must be reserved for future publication. Helpful studies already in print include *GOD WHO ACTS* (SCM/1952) by George Ernest Wright and Richard R. DeRidder's *DISCIPLING THE NATIONS* (Baker/1974).

The comment about the leadership of Woodrow Wilson may be found on page 20 of his *LIFE* by Josephus Daniels (Johnston/1924).

CHAPTER 2/REASONS FOR REFOCUS

In this chapter, much of the reference information has come to me orally through numerous seminars in church growth. We may be rapidly reaching a crisis if the current attrition in the preaching ministry continues. Meanwhile, laymen are just as frustrated in another way. Rather than work through the problems, many laymen and preachers are simply throwing up their hands.

Kenneth Chafin's *HELP, I'M A LAYMAN* (Word/1966) is a down-to-earth account of what happens when a preacher becomes a layman again. It is the author's personal story of moving from the pulpit to the pew and the difference in perspective which follows.

Although the impotency of theory without action is mentioned by numerous philosophers, it is probably the American pragmatists who have landed the heaviest blows. *PRAGMATISM* (Longmans/1970) by William James provides some very productive background reading. Alfred North Whitehead criticizes education for being "overladen with inert ideas" (*AIMS OF EDUCATION*/Mentor Edition/1974/13).

Beyond the twentieth-century philosophers, one can return to the Scriptures and read the parable of Jesus about the wise and foolish builders. The wise man who built his house upon a rock represents those who believe and receive the truth. The man whose house collapsed *heard* what Jesus taught, but he did not *do* anything about it (Matthew 7:24-27).

One of the most fruitful sources for the section entitled "The Unfinished Work" is Adolph Harnack's monumental study, *THE MISSION AND EXPANSION OF CHRISTIANITY* (Harper Torchbook/1902). In chapter five especially, the author presents the strong contrast between the pagan and Christian attitude toward the weak and suffering.

I have been cautioned by some reviewers to avoid encouraging the kind of evangelism "which is not concerned about the reconciliation and salvation of the whole man." I heartily agree. The equipping-ministry concept is a key to the body of Christ ministering to its own members. It provides a way to free those gifts within the body which are so essential to its own upbuilding (Ephesians 4:16).

CHAPTER 3/MOVING TOWARD CHANGE

The philosopher Descartes mentions the jaundiced person who judges "everything to be yellow because his eye is tinged with yellow" (DESCARTES/Vol. 1/ Cambridge/44). All of us suffer from a similar malady in our thinking, to one degree or another. It is so difficult to "get outside ourselves" and take a new look at a different proposition or idea.

Several reviewers felt I should have provided more examples of churches which practice an equipping ministry. I suggest the readers consult the study of Oscar E.Feucht entitled, *EVERYONE A MINISTER* (Concordia/ 1973) and the numerous titles in the "Additional Readings" section. For a further discussion of the idea that the seminary can serve as a model for the congregation, see *THE GREENING OF THE CHURCH* by Findley Edge (Word/1971).

A frequent question emerging in Church Growth Seminars is simply, "Why do you expect the church to adopt an equipping ministry when it is very obvious that some congregations today with the fastest rate of growth have an autocrat in the pulpit?" My first response is to say simply, "The New Testament presents an equipping kind of ministry." My second is to point out that very few studies have been made about what happens to congregations after an autocratic minister is removed from the scene.

I take the long view in regard to a congregation and its vitality and growth. I not only want to know what is happening now, I also want to know what the health of this congregation is going to be two or three decades from now. Every major American city can furnish ample testimony about the thriving church yesterday which is practically out of business today. Many factors must be taken into account in order to explain the decline, but often the root of the problem is an autocratic minister who has failed to make any provision for the future. When he is gone, the congregation flounders without leadership.

CHAPTER 4/LIBERATION FOR ALL

We may soon witness strong expressions of anti-clericalism in this nation. America thus far has escaped the clergy revolt which one finds in France and Mexico. Many reviewers of this book, however, mention the growing tension between the pulpit and the pew in the United States.

Unfortunately, many of the "laymen's movements" have become a "criticize-the-preachers-league." A preaching minister in Wisconsin writes, "After traveling nine years with a National Board, I know for sure that many lay persons are restless to the point of mutiny. I would agree that we pastors are to blame."

With the renewed opportunities for ministry and outreach facing the church today, surely now is not the time for the pulpit and the pew to take aim at each other. Part of the thrust behind this chapter is the idea that we can all gain a renewed vision of ministry if we restudy the New Testament together. I believe much of the frustration being felt in the pew today can be traced to a preaching minister who thwarts the ministry of others instead of helping them. Christians in the pews want a genuine ministry, but they are tired of the "busywork" often assigned to them by preachers who try to keep members active with superficial projects.

Part of the problem is related to the power structures in the church. If we can transfer power-consciousness to task-consciousness, then the problem will begin to be resolved. Our focus must be upon the job which needs to be done, not upon getting our share of the credit for doing it. The ministry of the church then becomes a symphony rather than a solo. It must be said, though, that some church boards expect the impossible from a preaching minister and his family.

The quotation from Stephen Neill is taken from *HISTORY OF CHRISTIAN MISSIONS* (Penguin Books/ 1964/24).

CHAPTER 5/A PRACTICAL APPLICATION OF THE PRINCIPLE

This chapter is pivotal in this study. Many who are convinced of the validity of an equipping ministry are still unable to put the concept into practice. This section should provide some helpful ideas in getting started. Instead of trying to spell out all the ways a congregation can begin practicing the ministry of all believers, I have left plenty of room for a church to chart its own course at its own speed.

Although the congregation may begin its practice in a "church-type setting," I certainly do not expect the idea to end there. We need to see our own vocation itself, whether it is nursing, teaching, administrating, banking, or carpentering, as an expression of our ministry for Christ.

Many reviewers have responded in this chapter to the section on "sermonizing." One preaching minister writes, "I am convinced that the most critical and sometimes misspent opportunity for equipping is the Sunday morning worship service." Another says, "All the people being trained for hospital calling, ministry to shut-ins, calling on the lost, and other important phases of ministry, must also have the opportunity to use the pulpit for teaching." He suggests the following possibilities during worship:

1. Three-minute missionary reviews
2. A five-minute sermonette preceding the major message
3. A ten-minute talk on a phase of ministry in which the speaker is personally involved.

The brief section on the role of women in the church probably elicited more comments than any other. Some feel I have thrown the door of the church wide open for the women to take over all the leadership. Others think this section should be more fully developed in view of the far-reaching ministry of women. Still others think that my language throughout the study has a male prejudice due to the repeated reference to "he." One prominent church woman asked why it took me so long to get around to mentioning the role of women.

The "ministry of believers" involves both men and women. The role of both is the intended theme from the beginning of the book. Congregations will each have their own ways of enlisting the services of women. The church has been commissioned to take the gospel to the whole world. Within that broad framework, room exists for everyone to have a meaningful ministry—both women and men. On the Day of Pentecost when Peter announced the coming of the Spirit-age with, "your sons and daughters shall prophesy," he referred to the vital role of both men and women in the kingdom of God (Acts 2:17, 18).

The role of women in the church today is a very lively topic. Is anyone able to produce a study which carries the balance upon which everyone can agree?

CHAPTER 6/EQUIPPING OTHERS FOR MINISTRY

Although I am not a proponent of the theory that polity in American churches is simply a reflection of American political life, I have found the study of American presidents very interesting in view of the principle of an equipping ministry.

In the American Statesman Series, the biographer of Thomas Jefferson offers an important observation about the nature of his administration. The author says, "Jefferson never used the accent of command or assumed the bearing of a leader. . . . He simply communicated suggestions and opinions to this or that selected one among those who believed in him" (Morse/236).

In a discussion of the type of leadership which Theodore Roosevelt gave the nation, Samuel Eliot Morison notes the strong kind of personal appeal which "Teddy" made to the American people. Even Woodrow Wilson (who was president at the time of "T.R.'s" death) admitted America had lost the president she loved. Morison observes, however, "Yet in one respect Roosevelt failed as a leader. He inspired loyalty to himself rather than to his progressive policies; he neglected while he still possessed the power of patronage, to build up a progressive nucleus within the Republican party" (OXFORD HISTORY OF THE AMERICAN PEOPLE/III/153).

"The Living Stones" section in this chapter contains implicitly the institutional spin-off principle. Good institutions will always be spawning new institutions. The family moving away from an active home congregation will not languish somewhere in a far-off city. They will either find a church of their own liking or start a new one in their living room or a neighborhood school. One of the best books in this field is by Carl W. Moorhous. In his GROWING NEW CHURCHES (Order from LCC Bookstore/Lincoln, Illinois), the author explains how a handful of families can lay the foundation for a thriving congregation.

Regarding my discussion of "gifts," one wise reviewer wrote, "I have seen people informed by one congregation that they were wrong in understanding their gifts, only to have them move to another congregation and develop their gifts beautifully." The reviewer is obviously right. We have all made mistakes about the gifts of others.

The seminarian voted "most likely to succeed" by the faculty may be a dismal failure in the preaching ministry. On the other hand, the student who barely makes it may accomplish a significant and enduring work. In that mysterious realm of the human personality where the Spirit does His work, only God can predict with certainty the future development of spiritual gifts.

CHAPTER 7/HOPE FOR WORLD EVANGELIZATION

Much of the "laity literature" of the middle decades of this century is keyed to social action or makes a renewal thrust. The possibilities for world evangelization are often overlooked.

Strangely enough, some critics today see the wedding of the laity movement and world evangelization as a new kind of exploitation. The New Testament obviously presents a different point of view. The last recorded words of Jesus to His disciples include His instructions for them to be His "witnesses in Jerusalem and in all Judea and Samaria and to the end of the earth" (Acts 1:8).

We have probably overlooked the "renewal power" of evangelism. I have seen the lackadaisical seminary student "come alive" when he begins to reach out to people in the community who are in desperate spiritual need. I have known elders and deacons in churches who became spiritually sensitized through their efforts to help others find their way to Christ. Renewal and evangelism are Siamese twins who must remain joined in order to live.

Nothing I have read about the social and political impact of the gospel surpasses the perceptivity of the words by Woodrow Wilson which are inscribed above his place of interment in the Washington Cathedral:

> The sum of the whole matter is this, that our civilization cannot survive materially unless it be redeemed spiritually. It can be saved only by becoming permeated with the Spirit of Christ and being made free and happy of the practices which spring out of that spirit.

THE AMERICAN CHURCH GROWTH STUDY SERIES

The American Church Growth Study Series began in 1972 with the publication of *THE GROWING CONGREGATION* and its companion *STUDY GUIDE* by Lincoln Christian College Press.

A concept-changing book, *THE GROWING CONGREGATION*, has now been used by hundreds of churches. It is written about the basic idea that a non-growing congregation needs to take a sharp look at itself in light of patterns of growth in the New Testament. Consequently, it accents basic Biblical principles of growth which must be applied today for effective growing churches.

THE GROWING CONGREGATION, basically a content-oriented study, was joined in 1973 by an action-oriented book entitled *HOW IN THE WORLD?* Donald A. McGavran wrote the foreword.

This second study concentrates on the "how" in evangelism. It includes chapters on analyzing the community, making a witness-survey, and guidelines for presenting the gosepl to others. The appendix of this book contains details about the way a congregation can conduct its own "Care-Promise Service."

In 1975, Standard Publishing began producing the entire series. Also during that year, *HOW IN THE WORLD?* appeared in seven mini-books. Each book deals with a specific area of evangelism and provides a shirt-pocket size guide for on-the-job training. Standard also printed the Witness-Survey cards and the Care-Promise cards to accompany the series.

In 1976, World-Wide Publications made available a cassette series to accompany the American Church Growth Study Series. The series includes two major addresses and two seminars on church growth. These cassettes were sent out to all who registered for the National Consultation on Church Growth.

THE EQUIPPING MINISTRY and its STUDY GUIDE is the third book in the series. This book is published as an effort to help churches practice the ministry of all believers. It is written with the view that world evangelism is only an empty dream unless the preaching ministry can return to its primary task—equipping the saints for ministry. Below are a series of "steps" for implementing these studies in the congregation. Although I begin with THE GROWING CONGREGATION, a number of readers have suggested to me that the entire series should begin with THE EQUIPPING MINISTRY.

STEPS TO USING THE AMERICAN CHURCH GROWTH STUDY SERIES

a preliminary observation

Church growth often begins in the hearts and minds of a few committed Christians. Tired of the "business as usual" routine in many American congregations, a handful of Christians believe God wants the church to grow. With this firm foundation, coupled with a spirit of fervent prayer, they are looking for resources to help them.

The materials in the American Church Growth Study Series are now proven instruments in assisting congregations in church growth. Some congregations have doubled in size during one year by following these ideas. Others have shown substantial gains with a dramatic increase in new members. I suggest the following steps in utilizing this series.

step one

Set up a study class using THE GROWING CONGREGATION as a basic text. Your results will be multiplied if you use the WORKBOOK with each member. If the class meets during the traditional thirteen week Sunday-school quarter, plan to cover a chapter every two weeks. For example, present Chapter One the first week, ("Church Growth and the New Testament Congregations"). During the second week, fill out the *STUDY GUIDE* for that chapter (preferably outside the classroom). Then allow ample time for class discussion.

Remember, a congregation cannot operate from a viewpoint in church growth which it does not possess. These ideas must flow through the life of the church if you expect results.

step two

Plan a Care-Promise Service. See the Appendix of *THE GROWING CONGREGATION* and *HOW IN THE WORLD?* for instructions.

step three

Involve those who respond to the Care-Promise Service in a study of *HOW IN THE WORLD?* Begin your program of calling in the community. We have discovered through our studies that the best time to call for Christ in America is on Saturday morning from 10:00 to 12:00. The following schedule may be followed or adapted:

9:00 - 9:45	Instruction and Prayer
9:45 - 10:00	Assignments Given/Teams Chosen
10:00 - 12:00	Calling
12:00 - 1:00	Light Lunch and Report Session

It is probably not best to schedule a continuous program of calling without some letup. If you choose Saturday morning, for example, you might schedule eight weeks calling in the fall and another eight weeks in the spring. If your winters are inclement, you can schedule around the cold and rainy months if necessary (although some of the best calling I've ever done has been during a blizzard or rainstorm). A summer calling program can be fitted to the lifestyle of your congregation.

step four

Through the triple alliance of prayer, study, and action, your congregation should be well on the road to developing a genuine ministry of believers. *A calling program is only one congregational ministry.*

step five

In a smaller community, a thriving congregation may need to wait for a new harvest to develop.

That may be the time to move toward the goal of helping each member of the congregation develop his/her potential as a minister for Christ.

A study of THE EQUIPPING MINISTRY should assist the congregation in this endeavor. Help each member of the class find a meaningful ministry during the period of study. Once again all your efforts will be multiplied if you use the STUDY GUIDE.

step six

Remember, new Christians often become the most zealous workers in the harvest fields of the Lord. Help them develop their gifts from the Holy Spirit for the work of Christ. Let them join the multiplied thousands who are praying and working daily for strengthened and growing congregations.

ordering information

The entire American Church Growth Study Series is available by writing to: STANDARD PUBLISHING, 8121 Hamilton Avenue, Cincinnati, OH, 45231. Telephone: 513/931-4050.

The same series with cassettes is available from WORLD WIDE PUBLICATIONS, Box 1240, Minneapolis, MN, 55440. Telephone: 612/336-0940.

RESOURCES FOR
AMERICAN CHURCH GROWTH

INTRODUCTION

For extensive readings in the field of American Church Growth, I suggest that the student turn to the Church Growth Bibliography section in the *KEY 73 CONGRE-GATIONAL RESOURCE BOOK* which is available in most libraries.

Since this bibliography was published, a number of authors have made contributions to the field. Some of them are included in this group. These materials should be added to the KEY 73 listing. Again, as I stated in *HOW IN THE WORLD?* my mention of a book does not mean I agree with all of the author's conclusions.

a

The most comprehensive study of religion in America to appear recently has been made by Sidney E. Ahlstrom, entitled *A RELIGIOUS HISTORY OF THE AMERICAN PEOPLE* (Yale/1972). It is an invaluable investigation, I believe, for getting an historical perspective for church growth in America.

Wilbur R. Aten's little booklet *THE GREAT COMMISSION FESTIVAL* tells how to combine the ideas of "Faith-Promise" and "Care-Promise" in the congregation. Write to NCGRC, Box 3760, Washington, D.C., 20007, for a sample.

Win Arn has produced several professionally-made films, including "And They Said It Couldn't Be Done" and "How to Build a Church." He is also the editor of the magazine *CHURCH GROWTH: AMERICA*. Write to IACG, 333 East Foothill Blvd., Arcadia, CA, 91006.

b

Howard A. Ball is producing useful materials to help congregational growth. Write to Churches Alive! Box 3800, San Bernardino, CA, 92413.

Mr. Wendell Belew has contributed several fine studies to church growth literature. One of these is entitled *CHURCHES AND HOW THEY GROW* (Broadman/1971). Another book he compiled is called *MISSIONS IN MOSAIC* (Broadman/1974). It contains an account of mission work among America's various ethnic groups.

Paul Benjamin is developing the American Church Growth Study Series. Designed to help congregations grow, the series thus far includes *THE GROWING CONGREGATION*, *HOW IN THE WORLD?* and *THE EQUIPPING MINISTRY*. Study Guides are also available. Write Standard Publishing, 8121 Hamilton Ave., Cincinnati, Ohio, 45231.

A National Bicentennial Committee has published ten Study Guides which can be very useful in equipping an every-member ministry. The authors and titles are:

    (1) Knofel Staton, *PERSONAL BIBLE STUDY*
    (2) Wayne Shaw, *DESIGNING THE SERMON*
    (3) Eleanor Daniel, *TEACHING*
    (4) Charles L. Lee, *SHEPHERDING*
    (5) Paul Benjamin, *CALLING FOR CHRIST*
    (6) Carl Moorhous, *NEW CHURCH PLANTING*
    (7) Bruce Parmenter, *COUNSELING*
    (8) Woodrow Phillips, *MISSIONARY PROGRAMMING*
    (9) Knofel Staton, *DISCOVERING MY GIFTS*
   (10) Gordon Clymer, *FAMILY WITNESSING*

These studies may be obtained for $1.25 each by writing to "Equipping an Every-Member Ministry," Box 39073, Cincinnati, OH, 45239. A check or money order must accompany your order. Many of these Study Guides could serve as a basic text for the SUGGESTED COURSE OFFERINGS in the Appendix.

Gerald L. Borchert has written *DYNAMICS OF EVANGELISM* (Word/1976), a very timely Biblical study of evangelism.

Bill and Vonette Bright have both made valuable contributions in the evangelistic field. Dr. Bright's books include: *REVOLUTION NOW!* (Campus Crusade/1970) and *COME HELP CHANGE THE WORLD* (Revell/1970).

Mrs. Bright serves as National Coordinator for the Great Commission Prayer Crusade (Arrowhead Springs, San Bernardino, CA, 92414), an organization dedicated to the ministry of prayer. *PRAYER HANDBOOK, Vol. I,* is rich with information about helping people pray. Write for additional materials.

c

Robert E. Coleman is responsible for a series of Biblical and evangelistic studies. One of his latest contributions is *EVANGELISM IN PERSPECTIVE* (Christian Publications, Inc./1975). He has also written several small Bible lessons published by Revell entitled *LIFE IN THE LIVING WORD*, and *THE SPIRIT AND THE WORD*.

Kenneth L. Chafin, Chairman of the American Lausanne Committee, has recently published a series of messages on evangelism entitled *THE RELUCTANT WITNESS* (Broadman/1974). Each message contains the author's rich insight regarding a case-study in the New Testament.

N. Dale Cluxton is a Christian leader deeply dedicated to the principle of the equipping ministry. Write to 604 Holt Avenue, Englewood, OH, 45322, for an order blank listing his materials.

J. E. Conant's earlier study *EVERY MEMBER EVANGELISM* is now available through Harper and it has been completely updated by Roy F.Fish.

d

A series of Biblical studies available for homes and schools are coming from the pen of John F. DeVries. Samples of these stimulating and well-illustrated studies are available by writing to WHBL, P. O. Box 11, South Holland, IL, 60473.

Broadman Press has recently reprinted a book by Lewis A. Drummond, now entitled *LEADING YOUR CHURCH IN EVANGELISM*, an important study text. The author is also responsible for a comprehensive bibliography on evangelism in MS form. Write to 2825 Lexington Road, Louisville, KY, 40206.

Using Maxie Dunnam's *WORKBOOK OF LIVING PRAYER* (Upper Room/1974), is a good way to help churches begin utilizing the often untapped reservoir of prayer.

e

Joe Ellis is responsible for *READY, SET, GROW*, thirty outlines for sermonic presentation, and *THE PERSONAL EVANGELIST* (1964), a study-book approach on ways of presenting the gospel to others in the community. Both books are available through Standard Publishing.

The French writer, Jaques Ellul is well known for his Biblical and cultural studies. Of particular interest is *THE*

PRESENCE OF THE KINGDOM (Seabury/1967). Other studies of Prof. Ellul include *THE MEANING OF THE CITY, PRAYER AND MODERN MAN*, and *THE JUDGEMENT OF JONAH*.

f

A recent study by Leighton Ford is called *NEW MAN . . . NEW WORLD* (Word Books/1976). Another excellent book by this author is his *CHRISTIAN PERSUADER* (Harper/1966). The evangelist makes a well-balanced approach to Christian outreach as it penetrates the entire spectrum of a society.

g

Gene A. Getz has contributed a very fine study entitled *SHARPENING THE FOCUS OF THE CHURCH* (G/L Publications/1975). Billy Graham writes books from an evangelistic viewpoint which sell in the millions. One of his latest, *ANGELS, GOD'S SECRET AGENTS* (Doubleday/1975), has helped revive an interest in the supernatural on the positive side. Andrew W. Greeley has made many contributions to the study of religion, including *THE DENOMINATIONAL SOCIETY, A Sociological Approach to Religion in America* (Scott, Foresman and Company/1972). Hollis L. Green looks at church growth from the reverse side in his *WHY CHURCHES DIE* (Bethany Fellowship/1972).

From the statistical viewpoint, The Glenmary Research Center, 4606 East-West Highway, Washington, D.C., 20014, has produced maps and studies which are available by writing. For a background in "pre-evangelism," get a copy of *THE DUST OF GOD* by Os Guinness (InterVarsity Press/1973.)

h

John F. Havlik has written a study entitled *THE EVANGELISTIC CHURCH* (Nashville/Convention Press/1976). Ideal for small group studies, this fine book joins his previous works, both by Broadman, *OLD WINE IN NEW BOTTLES* (a series of evangelistic addresses dedicated to young people) and *PEOPLE-CENTERED EVANGELISM*, a study pointing to the significance of leadership in the pews for evangelism.

Judith L. Best is responsible for sending me *EVANGELIZATION TODAY* by Bernard Haring (Fides Publishers, Inc./1974). This study represents an approach to evangelism from the standpoint of moral theology.

The first two volumes of a four-volume set entitled *GOD, REVELATION AND AUTHORITY* (Word/1976), have recently emerged from the penetrating pen of Carl F. H. Henry. Undergirding all the evangelist does is his fundamental concept of authority. This study, the author's *magnum opus*, should be background reading for any serious student working in the field of American church growth.

Melvin L. Hodges has written *A GUIDE TO CHURCH PLANTING* (Moody/1973) with practical information about establishing mission churches in addition to his earlier studies, *GROWING YOUNG CHURCHES, BUILD MY CHURCH*, and *CHURCH GROWTH AND CHRISTIAN MISSION*.

DIVISION IN THE PROTESTANT HOUSE (Westminster/1976) is the title of a well-researched report on intra-church conflicts in America. Dean R. Hoge is the primary author.

C. B. Hogue is responsible for a unique evangelistic book entitled *LOVE LEAVES NO CHOICE*. The book is sub-titled, *Life-Style Evangelism*. The first section of each chapter contains the author's personal experience in evangelism, followed by an exposition of special themes. Richard K. Hudnut raises the problem of "quantity versus quality" in his *CHURCH GROWTH IS NOT THE POINT* (Harper/1975).

k

In *WHY CONSERVATIVE CHURCHES ARE GROWING* (Harper/1972), Dean M. Kelly points out the significant relationship beteen meaning and growth.

A very significant author in the field of the equipping ministry is W. Carl Ketcherside. Of special interest is his volume entitled *THE ROYAL PRIESTHOOD* (Mission Messenger/1956). Write to 139 Signal Hill Drive, St. Louis, MO, 63121, for a list of the author's additional works.

Charles W. Koller's *POINTERS FOR PASTORS* (Crescendo/1974) contains many helpful hints on evangelism.

BEYOND THE EITHER-OR CHURCH (Tidings/1973) is a study by Alfred C. Krass. In it, the author decries a fragmented kind of evangelism which divides people into "souls" and "bodies." He calls instead for an "incarnational evangelism" which is aware at all times of the world in which we live.

Nate Krupp has written *YOU CAN BE A SOUL WINNER* (Lay Evangelism/1962) and *A WORLD TO WIN* (Bethany/1966). Both books contain a very practical approach for teaching laymen how to witness, by an author who is a veteran in the field.

l

CHURCH GROWTH: EVERYBODY'S BUSINESS (Standard Publishing/1976), by Dr. E. LeRoy Lawson and Dr. Tetsunao Yamamori, gives answers to such questions as: Why should I evangelize? Why don't all churches grow? Who should be a missionary? Every phase of church growth is covered in four chapters.

LET THE EARTH HEAR HIS VOICE (World Wide Publications/1974), the official reference volume with papers and responses from the International Congress on World Evangelization, is tremendously important for the student who wants to obtain a "feel" for church growth in its global implications.

Harold Lindsell's THE BATTLE FOR THE BIBLE (Zondervan/1976) raises the important issue of Biblical authority.

m

The most prolific writer of published material in the field of church growth is probably Donald A. McGavran. (A. R. Tippett may be the most prolific writer of material still to be published.) The author's earlier materials reflect his missionary heritage. More recently, he has turned his attention also in the direction of American church growth. HOW TO GROW A CHURCH (G/L Publications /1973) is a book of conversations between Win Arn and Donald A. McGavran. The latter's UNDERSTANDING CHURCH GROWTH (Eerdmans/1970), now in paperback, is being followed as a textbook in many American seminaries. The case-studies, taken largely from outside the United States, have a powerful application for the American scene, especially in regard to equipping laymen to minister. Many Christians overseas are far ahead of Americans in this respect.

The Missions Advanced Research and Communications Center (MARC), 919 W. Huntington Drive, Monrovia, CA, 91016, is responsible for a series of "Profiles" on the status of Christianity in numerous countries. One is available for the United States.

Matthew M. Meyer has prepared a little booklet on *Visitation Evangelism* available at 1451 Dundee Avenue, Elgin, IL, 60120.

Full of lively illustrative material is *HOW TO TELL A CHURCH* (Tidings/1975) by Danny E. Morris. It has real value in helping a congregation "open up" in regard to its problems and opportunities. The author has also written *A LIFE THAT REALLY MATTERS, THE INTENSIVE CARE UNIT,* and *ANY MIRACLE GOD WANTS TO GIVE.*

n

WHAT'S GONE WRONG WITH THE HARVEST? (Zondervan/1975) by H. Wilbert Norton and James Engel provides a synthesis between church growth and communications in a strategy for evangelism.

o

J. Edwin Orr has spent a lifetime studying revivals around the world. Included in the works from this prolific author are *CAMPUS AFLAME* (Regal/1971) and *THE FLAMING TONGUE,* sub-titled, *The Impact of the 20th Century Revivals* (Moody/1973). The author's studies are well researched and fully documented. He is currently preparing to publish a series of books which will probably provide the most comprehensive study of revivalism in print.

p

PROCLAIMING THE DOCTRINES OF SALVATION (Broadman/1975) is a series of evangelistic messages compiled by James A. Ponder. The sermons are from well-known preaching ministers. Jaroy Webber wrote the foreword.

q

A member of the Academy for Evangelism in Theological Education, Ralph W. Quere, has published a study reflecting the Biblical roots for the "Message Medium" and "Mission Method" of evangelism. It is entitled, *EVANGELICAL WITNESS* (Augsburg/1975). A brief study-guide by Harold H. Zietlow is also available.

r

T. A. Raedeke has edited a report on the impact of Key 73. Named *YESTERDAY, TODAY AND FOREVER* (Canon Press/1974), it contains articles by Carl F. H. Henry, Harold Lindsell, Leighton Ford, and Thomas A. Zimmerman. (Although some have the tendency to disparage the Key 73 effort, I personally feel it will be looked upon by historians of evangelism in America as one of the major turning points in the twentieth century.)

Lawrence O. Richards has contributed a popular study called *A NEW FACE FOR THE CHURCH* (Zondervan/1970). The author approaches the growth of the church from his background in Christian education.

s

The works of Lyle Schaller are coming into increasing prominence in the church growth movement. For those who are especially interested in studying church growth from the viewpoint of the local congregation, his works offer invaluable insights. Of particular value is his book, *THE DECISION-MAKERS* (Abingdon/1974) as well as *PARISH PLANNING* (1971), *THE PASTOR AND THE PEOPLE* (1973), and *CREATIVE CHURCH ADMINIS-TRATION* (1975). This latter book was co-authored with Charles A. Tidwell.

YOUR CHURCH HAS REAL POSSIBILITIES (G/L Publications/1976) is by the American church growth visionary, Robert H. Schuller.

Charles Shaver holds a deep concern for the conservation of new lives in Christ. He writes from the twin perspective of his post in a seminary and as a member of a Kansas City congregation. Beacon Hill has published his manual and study packet entitled *CONSERVE THE CONVERTS* (1976).

Silas Shotwell is responsible for an evangelistic notebook with four messages on cassettes. Called *DYNAMICS FOR EVANGELISM*, it is available from Good News! Publications, P.O. Box 13507, Fort Worth, TX, 76118.

t

From a revivalistic perspective, Charles R. Tarr has written *A NEW WIND BLOWING* (Warner Press/1972). The author presents a personal account of what has been termed "The Anderson Revival."

w

A former missionary who is now devoting much of his energies to church growth in America is C. Peter Wagner. His book *YOUR CHURCH CAN GROW* (G/L

Publications/1976) is a development of his lectures on church growth in America. Also in 1976, the author produced a study-notebook with twelve classroom lectures on cassettes. The materials may be worked through for seminary credit. (*UNDERSTANDING CHURCH GROWTH* by Donald McGavran is the basic text for the course.) Write to FEA, Box 989, Pasadena, CA, 91102. Some of the writer's previous studies include *A TURNED-ON CHURCH IN AN UPTIGHT WORLD, STOP THE WORLD—I WANT TO GET ON*, and *FRONTIERS IN MISSIONARY STRATEGY*.

John Wesley White presents some striking parallels between today's news events and Christ's return in *RE-ENTRY* (Zondervan/1971), probably his best-known work. The author's firm grasp on the Bible and current events is also underlined in his *FUTURE HOPE* (Creation House/1973), *THE RUNAWAY* (Crescendo/1976) and *WORLD WAR III* (Zondervan/1977).

y

Two authors who have worked through much of the material in Church Growth are Tetsunao Yamamori and E. LeRoy Lawson. They have written *INTRODUCING CHURCH GROWTH* (Standard/1975) and *CHURCH GROWTH, EVERYBODY'S BUSINESS* (Standard/1976).

Robert F. Yawberg, President of Prayer-A-Gram Foundation, Inc., has developed a unique ministry of prayer. Write to Box 8127, Station D, Fort Wayne, IN, 46808, for samples of materials.

CONCLUSION

The literary output in Church Growth is one of the most encouraging signs of our times. I taught evangelism in the seminary classroom at a period in American history when it was necessary to scour the landscape in order to find suitable texts. That period is over, at least for the present. There has never been a great movement in history without literature. Thank God today for the wonderful turnaround in this field. As the result of these literary labors, I pray that millions who are spiritually disenfranchised will come to know Jesus Christ as Lord and Savior.

"After this I looked, and behold a great multitude which no man could number . . ." (Revelation 7:9).